To Lead Is To Serve

Surrender =
Joining the winning side

"make Love your aim"

To Lead Is To Serve

How to

Attract

Volunteers

and Keep Them

℘

Revised and Updated

Shar McBee

With gratitude,

this book is dedicated to the one

who taught me

what it means to serve and

who showed me the joy

in all creation.

℘

Design by Kathie Kemp

Cover design by Paul Van Deusen

Cover photo by Susan Bransfield

Edited by Terry Hiller

Printed in the United States of America.
Library of Congress No. TXU 574 712
ISBN 0-9638560-2-2

Contents

Acknowledgments

Thank you to all the volunteers, organizations, and volunteer leaders who use *To Lead Is To Serve* in your lives. Thank you to Garrick Colwell for your encouragement to expand *To Lead Is To Serve* into new directions. My grateful appreciation to Terry Hiller for your extraordinary editing and insights. And a special thank you to the following advisors and friends for generously sharing your wisdom, encouragement and your expertise:

Robert Allen, Maggie Augello-Luke, Beatriz Betanzos, Wendy Biro-Pollard, Sandra Bloodworth, Shelley Brandes, Cathy Butler, Sarah Canright, Liz Carpenter, Charles & Rolinda Carrington, Edna Ching, Mark & Sandra Cohen, Luci Comparelli, Bob & Brenda Cooke, Deborah DeWitt, Patty Solo Downs, Bill Eastman, Susan Ellis, Kekoa Enomoto, Avi Farzan, Chris Forsyth, Bill & Carol Gordean, Chinmayi Gorzen, Giuliana Haim, Lisa Haim, Mark Victor Hansen, Wendy Hee, Mike Herb, Caroline Hermans, Cathy Herzog, Ralph Hilton, Alison Hoornbeek, Jim Hornfischer, Spencer Johnson, Inese Kaufman, Chris Kemp, Kathie Kemp, Indu Kline, Martha Koock Ward, Antoinette & Geoff Lindsey, Shyamala Littlefield, Mary Ann Lombardo, Edwardo Longoria, Leon Lowenthiel, Andrea Mann, Stephanie Marrack, Mary Ann Masur, Helen Maxie, Linda Mikkelsen, Jerome Navies, Jan Nellen, Suze Orman, Dona Pope, Clive Prout, Phylicia Rashad, Rita Ross, Leonard Saphier, Willa Scott, Sissy Sierro, Bob Sims, Peter Sitkin, Anne Strick, Lynn Tietjen, Kathy Travers, Janet Waring, Saul Waring and Lisa Werner.

Before You Begin

Welcome to the revised edition of *To Lead Is To Serve — How To Attract Volunteers & Keep Them*. You'll find new anecdotes in this publication, as well as new insights and new ways for you to work with volunteers and thrive.

Since the first edition was published in 1994, thousands of organizations have applied the *To Lead Is To Serve* principle and increased their volunteers significantly, some as much as 500%. I am grateful that the book is contributing to the advancement of so many wonderful causes.

A lot is happening in the *To Lead Is To Serve* world and you are invited to participate. There are weekly leadership tips, book discussion groups, "Learn by Phone" classes, video tapes, and new audio tapes. With my great-hearted business partner, Garrick Colwell, I am certifying additional *To Lead Is To Serve* seminar leaders. There might be one in your area, or perhaps you'd like to become one yourself.

In my speaking engagements, I get to meet the best people in the world, the generous ones who are making the world a better place. Perhaps we've met at one of these engagements, or we will.

You can learn more about our programs on the last page of this book, or contact me through the website. I'd love to hear from you.

If this is your first copy of *To Lead Is To Serve*, welcome and congratulations. You are on your way to discovering your own natural leadership style. If you are a returning reader, welcome back. Thank you for reading this book, thank you for caring about volunteers, and thank you for making the world better because you are in it.

How to Use *To Lead Is To Serve*

This book is for people with big hearts and high hopes who want to give of themselves to the world.

To Lead Is To Serve is an ancient leadership principle. It holds the key to attracting volunteers and keeping them. The book also contains the nuts and bolts that will make your life as a volunteer leader easier. Because the work of influencing people is gradual, the information in this book is designed to be implemented gradually, step by step, for lasting success.

Begin by taking one step at a time and applying it. As soon as you do, you will begin to see results. In a month, take the next step. In another month, take the next. In one year, your organization can be transformed.

One word of warning: none of these techniques will succeed if applied only once. Like brushing your teeth, each one must become a daily routine.

How *To Lead Is To Serve* Made My Life Easier

I began volunteering at age eight, answering the telephone at my church. I loved it and continued to volunteer throughout my life, while I was a teacher and later while I was a journalist. Since I had never been in charge of any co-workers, I found volunteer leadership to be a struggle. It was exhausting to get people to donate, get them to volunteer, and get them to participate.

Then I volunteered for a foundation where, after a few years, I found myself supervising up to 500 people. Many of them spoke languages different from my own. The foundation sponsors programs and seminars on seven continents in over fifty countries. We traveled all over the world, often arriving in a place only a few days before an enormous event. We had to find out where the program was, where the hundreds of volunteers and staff were, meet with them, train them, and then open the doors.

There was a wonderful supervisor who encouraged us to always give our best. No matter how impossible things seemed, she asked us to give our all. Long before I had heard of quality management, I was being stretched beyond imagination as I went from supervising no one to supervising people from pay phones or hotel room offices around the world. I was continually amazed at how it all worked, and how by giving my best, so much was accomplished. Years later, I was introduced to the concept which makes up the heart of *To Lead Is To Serve*. I thought, "That's the secret! In order to lead people, we must learn to serve them." It was exactly what I had learned from my supervisor.

When I reflect back on that time, it is amazing how volunteer work transformed my life and taught me how to work with others. For example, during my journalism career, I had always had an "attitude" toward public relations people. I believed that journalists were superior because we told the truth while they sold their clients. You can imagine my dismay when my supervisor expanded my duties to include overseeing public relations. It was the last thing I wanted to do. I cringed at the thought, but I began doing P.R.

In 1984 we were planning a nine-city tour of America. We would offer programs to thousands of people. At the end of one of the planning meetings, someone asked, "Would we like P.R. on this tour?" The consensus was, "Yes."

Then the tour manager asked, "What kind of P.R. would we like?"

One person said, "Not the kind that Shar does."

Whew! I didn't know what the person meant and I felt badly, but at the same time I was relieved that I would not have to do the public relations. Then, a couple of weeks later, I was on an airplane headed west to the first big city in advance of the tour. My job? Being in charge of P.R.!

I kept pondering, "Not the kind of P.R. Shar does. What does that mean? What kind do I do?" I really had to think about it. Eventually, I came to understand that I viewed P.R. work as a way to get something: get an article, get a cover story, get free publicity, get a public service announcement, get a calendar listing. Get. Get. Get.

It finally dawned on me that public relations is like any relationship. It does not work when you focus just on what you want to get. When you try to get something from people, they feel it and pull back. A good relationship is also about giving, about offering. In volunteer work, as in business, we offer our product. We offer our programs to anyone who is interested. We offer information. We offer courses. We offer volunteers the opportunity to participate.

Whenever my supervisor met with people, at the end of the meeting she offered them candy. I took that image and began thinking of volunteer work as offering candy to people. If they wanted it, that was splendid. If they did not, that was fine, too. It was definitely not the kind of public relations that I would have done before.

During the next eight years, this wonderful supervisor taught me many valuable secrets about working with volunteers. They were about how to achieve without pulling others down – how to be like the sun, which rises every morning flooding the darkness with light without denigrating the night. I learned that we do not have to be angry at a system to uplift it, and that without being gullible we can be fun loving and free. In short, I learned the secrets that can make any organization flourish.

How You Can Benefit From This Book

In ancient times everyone learned from a mentor. Today it is unusual when someone takes an interest in our growth. I am very grateful to my supervisor for mentoring me. If you are one of the fortunate ones who has had a good instructor in volunteer leadership, be grateful.

A sage once asked, "What is a human being's greatest support?"

The answer was "Gratitude."

So, before you begin, express gratitude for what you have learned and for those who have taught you.

Your gratitude will support you in expanding your knowledge.

The next thing to do is to take a moment and ask yourself, "What is my goal in reading this book?" Be specific. If it is to recruit volunteers, how many? If it is to attract a definite type of volunteer, what kind? If you are not certain about your goal, ask yourself, "Will this goal meet my organization's needs?"

I have a dream.
Dr. Martin Luther King

Create a colossal goal. You are serving the deserving. Why not do it in a big way? If you could wave a magic wand, what would you choose? Make that your goal! When you are satisfied with your choice, write it down where you can see it everyday. Also, write it on the first page of a notebook. As you continue reading *To Lead Is To Serve*, always have the notebook and a pen close by for working the exercises and jotting down your inspirations.

Many of the ideas suggested in *To Lead Is To Serve* will be new; others will be ideas you are familiar with or have an intuitive knowledge of. You might say, "Oh, I know that." However, knowing and doing are not the same. To attract volunteers and keep them, it is not enough to know how – you have to do it. You have to apply your new knowledge. This is the purpose of the exercises. Each one is designed to combine a principle with what you already know and apply it for successful results. So, as you read, when you come to an exercise, stop and do it!

The ideas in this book are to be implemented gradually, over one year, one step at a time. Often, that which arises suddenly dies suddenly, too. Quick changes can dwindle into nothing. So, let your knowledge evolve and grow continuously. Go through the book step by step. Concentrate on one chapter each month, letting the ideas and principles in it permeate your work and that of your organization. When all the steps are completed, start again.

While writing *To Lead Is To Serve: How to Attract Volunteers & Keep Them*, I interviewed 75 leaders who are in charge of many people. They are business executives, volunteer organizers, educators, politicians, and religious leaders. Together they have performed more than 1,500 years of volunteer service. I hope their wisdom and inspiration will serve you.

Shar McBee

1

To Lead Is To Serve

℘

I don't know what
your destiny will be,
but one thing
I do know:
the only ones among
you who will be
really happy
are those who have
sought and found
how to serve.

Albert Schweitzer

ℰ

The first step is to serve.

There is a story in the Talmud about a king and his son. They loved each other very much but they could not get along. So the son left home and went far away.

After a while, word came back that the son was not doing well. The king sent a message to the prince and said, "Come home."

But the prince was too proud. He sent a message back to his father, " I cannot."

Then the king sent another message saying, "Just turn around and come as far as you can. I will meet you wherever you are."

This story expresses the essence of what it means to lead by serving. If we want to lead, we must learn to serve.

When I first became a volunteer leader, I expected people to meet me where I was, to have the same level of commitment and the same interest in the project that I had. Sometimes I expected the volunteers to know everything they were expected to do, so I didn't even bother to train them. I found out it does not work that way.

People volunteer because they care. Our job is to make it possible for them to give as much as their hearts can give. This means to find where they fit, how their skills can be applied, and then to give them what they need to do the work. We have to meet them where they are. If we are the leader, we have to be like the king in the story.

To Attract Volunteers:
Meet Them Where They Are

The importance of meeting people where they are was first taught to me during a time when I was working on a large seminar. About 5,000 people showed up – many more than we expected. As the number of people increased, the ushers became overwhelmed and were not doing a good job of seating them quickly and courteously. They had been trained to treat each person respectfully but, as the crowd grew, they forgot that a crowd is still made up of individuals. Consequently, they were treating people like a herd of cattle, not human beings. My supervisor told me to do something about the situation.

I met with the ushers in a private room and began pointing out what they were doing wrong and what they should be doing instead. Later, the supervisor called me and asked, "What did you say to the ushers?"

I replied, "I pointed out how they should be doing the seating."

She inquired, "Did you ask them if they had eaten lunch?"

I was taken aback by her question. It never occurred to me to ask if they had eaten. However, later I saw that the ushers were under great strain with the big crowds and the last thing they needed from me was more pressure. What I was doing was like discovering a group of drowning people and offering them a swimming lesson. The ushers didn't need my instruction. They needed my support. They needed me to see the situation from their point of view. They also needed the energy that eating lunch would give them. This was an altogether new way of looking at the situation and I have never forgotten the lesson.

Before people can accomplish anything, their basic needs must be met. We, the ones in charge, must remember to give basic support, basic nourishment. We must look carefully at what volunteers need in order for them to do a good job and we must make sure that they get it. We must serve them in all ways. The experience with the ushers was a wonderful lesson for me in *To Lead Is To Serve* and meeting people where they are.

One pound of learning
requires ten pounds
of common sense to apply it.
Persian Proverb

Draw Strength from Ancient Wisdom

To Lead Is To Serve is an ancient and timeless leadership lesson. It has been stated in many ways and many languages throughout the ages.

The *I Ching,* a book of chinese wisdom, states, "To rule truly is to serve."

Saint Francis of Assisi said, "It is in giving that we receive."

The Upanishads, ancient scriptures of India, say, "If you want to be happy, be giving."

Jesus taught the lesson of *To Lead Is To Serve* saying, "The greatest amongst you is servant of all." Saint John describes how Jesus washed the disciples' feet and then said, "If I am your Lord and master, I have given you an example. If ye know these things, happy are ye that do them."

Today, Volunteer leaders who apply the *To Lead Is To Serve* principle report an increase in vigor, power and effectiveness. I find it exhilarating and it increases my capacity to serve. On days when things aren't going as I wish; when I feel stuck; when I think people aren't cooperating; if I ask myself, "How can I serve?" I immediately feel stronger and the situation improves. *To Lead Is To Serve* is a seasoned leadership principle that has worked since ancient times and it will work for you, too.

How to Prosper

Donations increase as an organization increases in volunteers. When an organization serves its volunteers, it prospers. One basic way of serving volunteers is giving them good supervision. Many organizations have only a part-time volunteer coordinator. Others pile so many responsibilities on the volunteer director that the time spent with volunteers becomes minimal. Presumably this is done to save costs, but it ends up costing the organization.

It has been shown that each hour given to supervising one volunteer yields nine hours in volunteer time. *You pay for one hour and you get nine hours free.* Still, good supervision and training are considered a luxury in most volunteer organizations even though the return on investment is so significant and brings such long-range benefits.

A state agency wanted to hire a full-time volunteer coordinator. In order to justify the cost to the legislature the agency conducted a study to determine the value of volunteers. The results showed that, in general, the benefits of volunteers were at least six times greater than the costs. For every dollar spent on supervising volunteers, six dollars in services were received from them. In terms of time alone, one hour spent by a staff member in supervising volunteers produced nine hours of volunteer work. The study showed that the benefits of supervising volunteers far outweighed the costs, in some cases as much as fourteen to one. As a result of the study, the state agency now has three paid staff members operating its volunteer program.

Using the *To Lead Is To Serve* method, you can train paid staff and volunteers to become outstanding supervisors. It has helped thousands of organizations to increase membership, donations and volunteer hours. When applied, this principle creates an energetic and loyal volunteer work force, which is priceless. It can significantly fortify your leaders and prevent burn-out. Using the *To Lead Is To Serve* guidelines will enable you to inspire volunteers to achieve beyond the call of duty. It will help them to release their creativity and remain loyal to your organization. *To Lead Is To Serve* can propel your organization beyond the survival mode and into prosperity.

Success with *To Lead Is To Serve* is Easy

To convert this principle into action is easy because it only requires a small shift in your thinking. Did you know that 98 percent of all communication is non-verbal? It takes place beneath the surface. If you are thinking, "What can I get out of these volunteers?" on a subtle level they will feel it and their natural tendency will be to put up a defense.

Instead, if you are thinking, "These people need something. What is it? How can I help?" invariably they will drop their resistance when they see your good intention.

Progress occurs when courageous,
skillful leaders seize the opportunity
to change things for the better.

Harry S. Truman

An instructor told me, "Volunteer leaders are usually cruel."

"Why?" I demanded, indignantly.

"Because they are willing to sacrifice people for the advancement of their cause."

To Lead Is To Serve makes it easy to advance your cause *and* your people. When volunteers know the leader cares about them, they will give their support to the cause. When they feel the leader only cares about the cause, they will withhold their service.

In any area of our lives, if we want something to improve, all we have to do is serve. If we want flowers to grow, water them. If we want youngsters to read, read to them. Isn't that the way things work?

Too often leaders adopt the point of view that because they are in charge, they are supposed to get something from people: time, allegiance, more work. *To Lead Is To Serve* says that when we are in charge, we are the ones who must give.

Work is love made visible.

Kahlil Gibran

John Feerick, Dean of Fordham Law School and Past President of the Association of the Bar of the City of New York is a tremendous advocate of *pro bono* (not for fee) legal work. He tells graduating lawyers: "You have received a lot of schooling, prestige, and respect. That makes you part of the aristocracy. You must recognize that what goes with that is a responsibility to be helpful to people who have problems dealing with the legal system and the law."

Improve Your Presentations

The principle of *To Lead Is To Serve* is so fundamental that it can be applied to any area of life and work. In any communication, if you hold the thought of service, your message will be received loud and clear.

This is particularly true in public speaking. Holding the thought, "I am here to serve" wards off fear and frees the communication to come from the heart. Magic occurs when a speaker shifts the focus away from herself and onto the audience. Stop worrying about, "What are they thinking of me? How am I doing?"

Instead ask, "What can I do for these people? How can I serve them?" Immediately you will connect with the audience.

Once, entertainer Phylicia Rashad was performing her nightclub act in Las Vegas. The act included a 16-piece backup troupe of singers, dancers, and band members. It was fabulous. Her character was completely different from the part she played on the successful television program, "The Cosby Show." One night, I attended both the early and late concerts and thoroughly enjoyed her performances.

The next day Phylicia and I were sitting around the pool planning some work we were doing together and talking about To Lead Is To Serve. Phylicia really liked the idea. Later that evening, at the early performance, she had the audience in her hand. They seemed to want to dance onto the stage with her. The show had been excellent the night before, but this time it was astonishing.

Backstage I asked Phylicia, "What happened? Why was it so much better tonight?"

She said, "I just kept thinking: 'How can I serve the audience?'"

Nothing in the show had changed. She sang the same songs and told the same jokes. It was an inner shift in her reasoning that made the difference. The first night she had wanted the audience to like her, to see that she is a good singer and a good dancer. The second night, instead of trying to get them to like her, she was thinking, "What can I give to these people? How can I make them happy? How can I serve them?"

Instead of thinking about herself, she was thinking about them.

Phylicia said, "These people came here for a good time. How can I help them have fun?"

That thought created a magical connection between the performer and the audience. The result was astounding. Her second show that night was even better. The band was so alive, it exploded and after the performance, they came backstage smiling and dancing. Phylicia said that this time she had been thinking, "How can I serve the band and the backup singers?"

To Lead Is To Serve. Phylicia Rashad was successful with it because she understood and applied the principle. You, too, can put the principle to work for your benefit. To do so is easy. To attract volunteers and keep them, resolve to serve them.

GEMS to
REMEMBER

℘

1
Meet people where they are.
The king and the prince.

2
Basic needs must be met.
Shar and the ushers.

3
To Lead Is To Serve is timeless and ancient.
St. Francis, the Upanishads, Jesus.

4
If you serve your volunteers, your
organization will prosper.
State agency study.

5
When volunteers increase,
the donations increase, too.
To Lead Is To Serve training.

6
To Lead Is To Serve only requires
a shift in your thinking.
I am here to serve.

7
Use *To Lead Is To Serve* to improve
your interactions.
Phylicia Rashad story.

EXERCISE
for SUCCESS

℘

1

Look over your appointments calendar.
Before each meeting you plan to
attend, ask yourself,
"How will I serve this group?"

2

Make a list of three volunteers.
Ask yourself,
"How can I serve these people?
What do they need
that I can give?"

3

Think of a volunteer who has let you down.
What can you do to serve
that person?

2

Be Welcoming

℘

CHAPTER TWO

Small cheer

and

great welcome

makes a merry feast.

William Shakespeare

ℰ

The second step is to be welcoming.

To feel welcome is wonderful, isn't it?

On the other hand, was there ever a time when you enjoyed feeling unwelcome?

Everyone wants to be recognized and greeted, to be included and to feel a part of the whole. To welcome another human being is a sign of respect and a great service.

In the fourth grade, I changed schools in the middle of the spring semester. The school year was almost over and neither the new teacher nor the students welcomed me with open arms. I felt like an outsider and changed from someone who loved school to someone who didn't. The result was that my grades plummeted. It was a relief when the semester came to a close.

All summer long I dreaded going back to school. When the first day of class arrived that fall, I was a very timid ten year old opening the classroom door and looking around at a room full of strangers.

Then a miracle happened.

A little girl smiled and waved and said, "Sit next to me." Her one gesture of welcome turned everything around for me. School was OK after all.

Welcoming is a powerful tool, yet it is so simple and obvious that it is often overlooked. Before we can attract new volunteers, we must keep the ones we have by continually welcoming them.

To Attract & Keep Volunteers –
Be Welcoming

At a luncheon sponsored by the Network of Volunteer Leaders, I sat across the table from a man who had conducted a survey to find out why volunteers continue to serve. He queried volunteers at a hospital, a social services organization, and a courthouse. The survey concluded that the most significant reason volunteers endured was that they received continuous recognition and appreciation from their immediate supervisor. The key words are "continuous " and "immediate." Welcoming requires the immediate supervisor to reach out to people on a regular basis.

Businessman Lex Brodie thinks that non-profit organizations would benefit from treating everyone like a customer. When I heard him say that, I recalled going to a non-profit with the intention of volunteering. People were moving about and talking to each other, but no one acknowledged that I was there. I waited ten minutes, then walked out. I didn't want to volunteer for an organization that didn't even notice me.

Brodie used to serve on the Hawaii Board of Education. After his election, he spent ten months visiting every school in the state. There are 239 schools in Hawaii and he sometimes visited one school several times, conversing with the principal, vice principal, teachers, staff, students, and parents. He said, "At many schools, I was the first member of the Board of Education these educators had ever seen on their campuses."

- Begin today to get to know the volunteers in your organization with whom you have never had a conversation.
- To keep volunteers, show interest in them and in their work by making each one feel respected, acknowledged and warmly welcomed on a regular basis.
- To attract volunteers, create a definite plan for letting every new person feel valued and needed.

Flourish with First Impressions

We only have one chance to make a first impression. Because first impressions are lasting, the way we welcome volunteers the first time will have a long-term effect.

Have you ever entered an office, been ignored by the receptionist, and watched someone else get a big smile from the same person? Did you feel like an outsider?

Or have you ever been ignored by the receptionist, waited a long time, and then been greeted by the salesperson like a long lost friend? This is disingenuous, not welcoming.

Everyone deserves to receive a warm greeting the moment they enter the door. Whether they are entering your establishment for the first time or the tenth time, they are entitled to be recognized with respect.

Joy Lewis, who is an officer in her political party, says she often discovers the best workers when they are standing alone. "If they have come to an event, it means they are interested. But if they don't know anyone, it is hard for them to get involved."

She recalls, "Once I saw a young man leaning against a wall at a pot luck. I introduced myself and it turned out he had just moved to this city and was looking for a way to become active. He became very involved with our organization after that.

"Someone has to take new people by the hand and introduce them around," Joy says.

Introductions are Significant

Introducing volunteers to others is an easy way to make them feel included and appreciated. It is hard to be enthusiastic about an organization when you are treated like an outsider. Introducing people to others makes them feel welcomed and a part of the group.

A true welcome includes proper introductions. When introducing two people, apply the principle of *To Lead Is To Serve*. The person making the introductions can serve the people who are being introduced by giving enough information about each one that a comfortable conversation can follow. It is not enough to simply say the two names and walk away. Too often in busy organizations the person making the introduction hurries through it so she can get back to the "real" work. If the goal of the organization is to succeed, making people feel welcome is the work.

A good introduction is a sign of respect. No matter what you think or feel about a person, she deserves your respect. When a person receives a respectful welcome, she will almost always want to keep volunteering.

> *I am prepared to meet anyone,*
> *but whether anyone is prepared for*
> *the great ordeal of meeting me*
> *is another matter.*

Mark Twain

Introductions benefit everyone. A young friend of mine recently began college in her hometown.

She had wanted to go away to school but for financial reasons had to enroll in the local university. She knew many of the students from high school, but instead of hanging out with them, she decided to try to meet people from out of town. She thought this would be more like going away to school. Every time she saw a student sitting alone, she introduced herself. Inevitably, she became the unofficial hostess of the first-year class, making lots of new friends and meeting people from far away. In this way, welcoming others helped her to get over her own disappointment about not going away to college.

It is said that one lake, by itself, gradually dries up. But when two lakes join they replenish each other. It is the same in an organization. People working together can refresh and vitalize each other. Friendly introductions help to create an atmosphere of warmth in which volunteers feel comfortable with one another.

There are many ways that you can incorporate introductions into your organization. At special events, officers and board members can make it a point to give a warm greeting and say hello personally to everyone in attendance. On a daily basis, one person can be assigned the duty of hosting and welcoming in the office or reception area. Create a list of staff and regular volunteers so that the host can make sure that new people meet everyone. The list can include some special interest or fact about each person in the organization. The host can introduce new people to others with similar interests.

Triple Your Attendance

When I first served on the Board of Directors of DOVIA, the Directors of Volunteers in Austin, Texas, our president's goal was to increase our membership. Attendance had been lagging at the meetings, so we did two things:

1. We asked each board member to say hello to everyone at every meeting and spend extra time with people the board member did not know.
2. We created "Greeters." These were five people who agreed to talk to every person at every meeting. The five wore badges saying, "Greeter," then each one recruited someone else to be a Greeter at the next month's meeting.

With this plan, everyone in attendance was assured of being welcomed by at least two people, a board member and a greeter. DOVIA met once a month and we initiated this welcoming policy at a June meeting. By August, we had tripled the attendance. Three times as many people were now attending our meetings!

None of this required extra time or extra money. The board members and the greeters were at the meetings anyway. Instead of talking to each other and visiting with old friends, they were reaching out to everyone.

An ex-president of DOVIA was at that August gathering. It had been awhile since she had attended one of our events and she was surprised to see so many people in attendance. She pulled me aside and whispered, "What happened to DOVIA?!"

People feel happiest when they feel they belong. Welcoming is a simple act that can create a major impact in any organization. However, it doesn't happen without forethought.

As a keynote speaker, I get to attend the conventions of many different volunteer organizations. At these events, the board of directors and officers will typically be introduced to the membership. When they are asked to stand, I like to watch where the board members are seated.

Are they sitting together or are they mixed in among the general membership? Ninety percent of the time, when they are introduced, the board members are sitting together.

It is a natural tendency to gravitate toward the familiar. That's why it is crucial to make a plan in advance to welcome everyone – new attendees as well as old. By consciously foregoing the familiar and seating themselves among those with whom they aren't normally in contact, board members and leaders can create a strong sense of welcome.

Many groups become adept at welcoming new faces and forget their faithful supporters. Remember to welcome the people who have been around a long time, too. They really count. They are the ones who will support your organization when the chips are down. It is amazing how a warm welcome from the executive director can breathe new life into a seasoned volunteer.

Telephone Smiles

On the telephone, a welcoming attitude can make or break a connection. The person who answers the telephone is more important than the CEO because that person creates the caller's entire perception of the organization.

To train everyone to have a welcoming attitude on the telephone, simply call a meeting of everyone who answers the phone. Ask them to consider these three questions:

1. How do they like to be received when they call an organization?
2. How do they react when a receptionist is not helpful?
3. How do they feel when someone pays attention to them?

A great discussion can ensue from these questions. Use the answers to create guidelines for telephone protocol.

How to Do a Lot with a Little

One small expression of welcome can have a long-term benefit. In the opening story of this chapter, a little girl welcomed me to the fifth grade by saying, "Sit next to me." Her four words meant everything and changed my whole experience of the new school. As a leader, you can change a volunteer's whole experience of volunteering for your organization with a few words of welcome.

When Jimmy Carter was running for President of the United States, he attended a dinner party in California. The hostess had arranged for guests to change seats after each course so that everyone would have the opportunity to sit next to Carter. It worked out that every guest except one woman sat next to him. At the end of the evening, the candidate made it a point to speak to this woman saying, "I'm sorry there wasn't one more course."

She said, "At that moment he won my support." During that election year she worked long hours for his campaign.

One easy step for doubling your chances of success: Be welcoming!

For advice on fundraising, visit my website www.JoyofLeadership.com

GEMS *to* REMEMBER

℘

1
Everyone wants to be included.
Shar's first day at school.

2
Welcoming includes reaching out
to people on a regular basis.
*The school board member
who visited every school.*

3
The way we welcome volunteers the first
time will have a long-term effect.
Being ignored by a receptionist.

4
Discover good volunteers when they are
standing alone.
The political party's pot luck dinner.

5
A true welcome includes proper introductions.
The young college woman who didn't go away to school.

6
Triple your attendance with welcoming.
DOVIA and the greeters.

7
It takes effort to overcome the natural tendency to gravitate toward the familiar.
Board members sitting together.

EXERCISE
for SUCCESS

1

How can your organization be
more welcoming? How can you be more
welcoming? When you have felt
welcomed, what created that
experience for you?

2

Is there a welcome sign?
Do people receive a warm, genuine smile
when they walk through the door?

3

Remember a time when you felt
unwelcome. How did it happen? Can you
prevent the same thing from happening
to others at your organization?

3

Appreciation

ℚ

CHAPTER THREE

Appreciation is
a wonderful thing.
It makes what
is excellent
in others
belong to us
as well.

Voltaire

ℒ

The third step is to express appreciation.

Ann Zyller arrived at my office discouraged. Months earlier, she had agreed to chair a fundraising dinner for an organization that we both volunteered for. Today, Ann wished she had never accepted the position.

"I can't get any support," Ann moaned as she flopped on the couch in my office.

"If you are looking for support," I suggested, "your greatest support is gratitude."

These words tumbled out of my mouth because I had made this statement in hundreds of speeches and seen it make a difference for hordes of volunteer leaders.

Ann wasn't convinced. So, I asked her to do an exercise that has worked wonders for countless organizations that I have worked with from churches to the Junior League. The exercise took only a few minutes, yet, when we were finished, everything had changed. Ann had recaptured her enthusiasm and both of us were energized.

We then had a brief discussion about the fundraising event and Ann left.

One month later, the event was a great success. The banquet hall was full of supporters; the organization raised a lot of money; and Ann was happy. She told me the exercise we did at my office was the turning point.

You can use the same exercise when you or one of your volunteers gets discouraged. Here's the exercise:

1. Make a list of five people you are grateful to.
2. Call each one and express your appreciation.

That's it.

The exercise takes very little time. You can rarely reach anyone in person, so it is mainly a matter of leaving voice mail messages. For Ann and me, it took less than fifteen minutes. She called five people and I called five. When we were finished, nothing had changed and yet everything had changed. Ann was no longer feeling unsupported. She was full of enthusiasm — for the organization, the people she had called and the fundraising dinner. The exercise refocused her attention. She was able to remember why she had accepted the position in the first place. This attitude made it possible for her to pass on her enthusiasm to others and gain the support she was seeking.

One of the people on my list to call was Burt. He had built a beautiful bookcase for the organization and every time I looked at it, I thought of him. So I gave him a call, leaving a message saying, "You put so much love into that bookcase. I want you to know I appreciate it."

Two weeks later, Burt's girlfriend told me, "He saved the message and re-plays it everyday."

Everyone wants to be appreciated.

Express your appreciation often. Once you begin, there are so many ways you can do this. You can develop a system for sending thank-you notes immediately and for calling volunteers regularly to acknowledge their good work. After I saw how energized Ann became when we called people to express our appreciation, I started adding another list to my daily "To Do" list. Now I write down what I have to do and next to it I make a "To Thank" list. I jot down the names of five people I appreciate and then I call them. This gives me lots of energy to start my "To Do's."

How Volunteers Bloom

In *To Lead Is To Serve*, the principle of appreciation recognizes that people volunteer for as many reasons as there are individuals. Behind each reason is a need. In order to express appreciation in a way that is truly effective, find out what each person's special need is.

A few years ago, I went to the dedication of an orchid garden. The speaker was the man who had established the garden. In his talk, he said that when he began the project he knew nothing about orchids and that in the process of growing the garden he had learned some valuable lessons.

Then he told the following story:

Through trial and error, he had learned that not all orchids are alike. He had found that some orchids could be thrown in a pile of sand and they would grow and bloom and blossom and be beautiful. He really liked these orchids. He did not have to do anything for them.

On the other hand, there were other orchids that he had to attend to several times a day. He had to mist, fertilize, coax, and talk to them in order to get them to grow. Still, they did bloom and they were beautiful.

When he said that, I thought, "Oh! That's just like people!" Some can be told what to do and they just do it. On their own, they accomplish their work wonderfully. Others, however, need attention, coaxing, and a lot of time in order for them to understand what needs to be done and then to do it. Others need praise. Then they flourish and they are magnificent. Not infrequently, the things that are the hardest to grow end up being really extraordinary (like children).

Volunteers are like rare orchids. Each one needs something different and when we are in charge we can serve them by giving them what they need. Like the gardener, we can "water" our volunteers. And like the king in the story from the Talmud, we can meet them where they are.

In busy organizations the leaders often get so involved in the work and trying to look good, that they forget to give volunteers what they need. They forget to do the watering. This is like the orchid gardener thinking that his job is to bloom and look gorgeous. No! His job is to take care of the orchids so that they can bloom. As the leader, we can be the one who does the planting, watering, and cultivation that help our volunteers to bloom. We don't have to worry about blooming ourselves. We can serve by making others look good.

Appreciation Increases Value

How can we increase the value of our staff and volunteers? One way is to appreciate them. When an investment appreciates, it goes up in value. It is the same with people. When we appreciate people, they recognize their own value and everything they do shines. Isn't it true? Tell your volunteers that you appreciate them and that others do, too.

The New York Philharmonic Orchestra gives out plaques as a way of expressing appreciation to its volunteers. The idea isn't original, but each one is inscribed with a message that is. Paula Root received a plaque that said, "In grateful recognition of her pioneering, gracious, and tireless work on behalf of the New York Philharmonic Orchestra." After years of arduous work as a fund-raiser, the plaque is still precious to her.

Just as everyone has special needs, each of us also has special aptitudes. Make it your challenge to meet people where they are and discover their strengths and talents. This is a powerful way of showing appreciation.

Mary Jane Anaya administers a community program for her state's judicial system. People who have been convicted of certain crimes can "do time" by offering service to this program. One young woman, 17, had been arrested three times. She had a severe truancy problem at school and had never fit in anywhere. So, imagine the surprise and delight of all when she blossomed as a volunteer. Mary Jane let the young woman choose how she wanted to serve. She helped her discover what she loves to do and then designed a program that fit this love with the needs of the organization. What a powerful way to acknowledge a young person and her special abilities.

The young woman became a "peer director" of five younger children whose problems were similar to her own. She chose to teach them kayaking. On their first trip, they ran into rough waters and the young woman bravely hooked five boats to her own and pulled them all to safety. It was the first time in her life that she had been responsible for anything or anyone and probably the first time that she had succeeded at something. She was on Cloud Nine.

Next, she planned a three-day campout for 13 younger children. This former truant and problem child who had failed every class in school, passed a difficult First Aid examination in order to be able to do her volunteer work.

This is a beautiful example of *To Lead Is To Serve.* Both the administrator and the young volunteer were leading by serving, and everyone benefited.

Look for ways to help each individual blossom. Every management book says the same thing: People who feel good about themselves do a better job. They take fewer sick leaves. They have more loyalty. They are more creative in their work. Just as we water orchids to help them grow, we can cultivate volunteers by offering our appreciation for the person and the work that he or she does.

There is a coach in Sydney, Australia, who knows how to appreciate even the least valuable players.

His team, the Manly Sharks, was fairly second-rate when he was hired as coach. One by one, he took the younger, weaker players aside and told them, "The other team members have confided in me that they really enjoy having you on the team. They like playing with you."

The result was that over the next two seasons the team totally transformed. It rose from the bottom of 25 teams to the top. Also, the players did not trade out to other teams, which is highly unusual. They loyally remained with the Sharks.

Your Timing Counts

To everything there is a season and
a time for every
purpose under heaven.

Ecclesiastes

Timing counts. This is true when giving praise and with just about everything. Give praise at the right time.

It is said that when people work for us we should show them our strength first and later show our sweetness. If we show our sweetness first, they'll walk all over us. This isn't a condemnation of people; it is a fact. We have to earn respect as leaders. If we don't earn respect, when we give our appreciation it won't be valued.

Appreciate volunteers when the time is right. Do not procrastinate! When we receive a bill for services rendered, we pay it. We do not like to pay the mortgage late, but we do put off telling someone, "Thank you." Why?

Jo Anne Matchette was a professional fundraiser for volunteer organizations in Wisconsin for 12 years. She says, "In all those years of fundraising I can count on one hand the gifts that were anonymous. Human beings like to be thanked and recognized."

According to Tony Proffit, who has been running successful campaigns in Texas for 25 years, "You have to get on the phone all the time – talking to people, thanking them. Write regular thank-you notes. Do not wait until you need something to contact them."

Former president of the Federation of Jewish Charities Peggy Tishman served on the Wellesley College Board of Trustees for a dozen years. Although she is retired from that board now, she admires and appreciates Wellesley for not forgetting her. She says, "I am always invited to events. Information is always disseminated to me. It makes an enormous difference. You never feel like now that you've done your stint, they've forgotten you."

She also gives Wellesley high marks for doing a super job with acknowledgements. One year, the goal was to raise $150 million. The volunteers surpassed it, raising $168 million. The college president came to a luncheon at Tavern on the Green in New York City to personally thank everyone who had helped to raise the money. Peggy says, "Now we can go back to any of those people because the thank you's were done so graciously."

Entice with Trust

Another way of appreciating people is to trust them. After you give volunteers something important to do, get out of the way and let them do it.

When he was running for Lt. Governor of Texas, Bob Bullock called together everyone who had ever worked for him, even those he had fired. He asked them to support his campaign in whatever way they wanted. They named themselves the "Bullock Alumni Raiders," placed newspaper ads, and had a big, nostalgic party that helped win Bullock the election.

There is a lot to learn from Bullock's willingness to trust other people's instincts, knowledge, and abilities. Anyone in a leader's position must have the wisdom to recruit people who are capable of directing others. This means selecting the right people and then allowing them to have a free hand. If we are too interfering, we may attract competent people, but we will never keep them.

It was always difficult for me to trust someone else to do the kind of job I wanted done. The only way I learned was by being thrown into a position that was too big for me to single-handedly control. I had no choice but to trust people. And do you know what? They were terrific!

When we let people exercise independent action, they will put forth more effort. When they do, however, we must not disappear into our own project. As the person in charge we must be there appreciating and reinforcing their hard work.

Strong volunteers need encouragement, too. If you are busy, you may assume that your strong volunteers can take care of themselves while you devote your time to those who need more supervision. Actually, you should do the opposite. Strong volunteers are like the steel in a building. They can carry a lot of weight, but if they fall, you lose it all.

I always thought I was a capable volunteer, but I was more capable when my supervisor was aware of what I was doing. Have you ever worked on a project that you knew you could do well and you had a lot of enthusiasm for, but you never heard from your supervisor? You received no input? When this happens to me, I begin to feel disconnected and unappreciated and my enthusiasm wanes. On the other hand, in a situation where my higher up is clearly aware of what I'm doing, involved, and interested – appreciating my work – I'm willing to go more than the distance to complete the project.

Supporting strong people brings long-lasting benefits. If the person in charge is wary of strong helpers, the organization will never grow.

One executive director complained to me that she could not find good volunteers. On closer examination, it became apparent that she did not make strong volunteers feel appreciated. She was assuming that they could take care of themselves and, on another level, she was intimidated by the competition. She liked her job and didn't want someone else vying for her position. She didn't share the responsibility. She held information secretly. The result was that the organization lost its strong people. Later, when a big project came up, there was no one to help.

When You Don't Want to Berate: Appreciate

A leader with the American Cancer Society had to speak to a volunteer he supervised about some inappropriate behavior. He resisted doing it, postponing the confrontation, but eventually he knew something had to be said. He didn't want to approach the volunteer with his own righteous indignation. He wanted to communicate the actual issues, not his own anger.

"Before the meeting," he recalls, "I contemplated everything that I appreciate about this woman. I made a list of all her great qualities and reminded myself of the many times she had been a fabulous volunteer."

"It worked," he exclaims. "It turned out to be very successful. Both of our concerns were covered and we parted peacefully."

Appreciating volunteers is a way of welcoming them. It must be done continuously, like polishing silver. There is a silver tray in my house that I look at every day. Occasionally, I get out the silver polish and shine the tray. Then, for awhile, it looks so brilliant that it catches my eye each time I pass by, giving me much pleasure. Inevitably, however, it becomes dull and needs polish again. I cannot claim credit for the silver in the tray. It was already there. The tray is beautiful on its own. But it doesn't shine unless I do the polishing.

Like precious metal, volunteers have an inherent value and beauty, but they need to be polished with appreciation again and again.

How do you attract volunteers and keep them? Genuinely and regularly acknowledge, applaud, thank, recognize, relish, admire, esteem, treasure, regard, love, honor, respect, and appreciate them.

Appreciating You

At the same time we are appreciating volunteers, we must learn to appreciate ourselves and our own contribution. We must truly appreciate the great work that we are doing.

Do you know what is needed in your organization? *You* are needed. So never forget how important you are.

Perhaps it is true in today's world that more people are working longer hours and fewer hours are spent volunteering. Perhaps more organizations are competing for the same volunteers. But does that make the work we are doing any less valuable? No matter how busy people may be, they are still looking for opportunities to enrich their lives.

Volunteer work is a priceless opportunity and a great gift to the world. Appreciate what your organization is contributing.

If you offer the Hope Diamond, will people turn it down because they are too busy? Unlikely. Keep this in mind when you offer someone the opportunity to volunteer.

For advice on fundraising, visit my website www.JoyofLeadership.com

GEMS to
REMEMBER

1
Gratitude attracts support.
The "To Thank" list.

2
Each volunteer's needs differ.
The orchid gardener.

3
Appreciate each volunteer's
strengths and talents.
The young kayak instructor.

4
Appreciation creates success.
The coach in Sydney, Australia.

5
Timing counts.
The Wisconsin and the Wellesley fundraisers.

6
After you give volunteers something to do, get out of the way and let them do it.
The Lieutenant Governor of Texas.

7
Appreciating volunteers must be continuous.
The silver polish.

EXERCISE
for SUCCESS

1

Write the names of three people who work with you and make a list of the things you appreciate about each one.

2

What kind of nourishment does each one need to help her do her work? A word of praise? A better piece of equipment? More or less responsibility? Some fun?

3

Write the names and the type of nourishment or appreciation that each one needs on a Post-It. Put it in your calendar for this week. Later, move the Post-It to next month, so you will remember to polish again and again.

4

Sacrifice

= sacred
Selfless Service
Karma Yoga
Surrender

get out of your head + into
your heart

Shed illusion
+
Delusion

☙

CHAPTER FOUR

If you want to
be given
everything,
give everything up.

Lao Tsu

ᢒ

.

The fourth step is sacrifice.

The entire earth revolves on the principle of sacrifice. Everything that is created comes from the sacrifice of something else. The seed sacrifices itself to the soil; the day sacrifices itself to the night; the wood sacrifices itself to the fire.

The word sacrifice means, "to make sacred." People often think of sacrifice as having to give something up, but it is nobler than that. When something is given up, a space opens for something else to evolve. Parents sacrifice for their children even though their efforts often go unappreciated. They give up a lot, but a human being evolves. Parents sacrifice themselves, then offer their sacred work to the world in the form of a child.

Have you ever known a company or a project to succeed when there was no sacrifice? To accomplish anything, first we must be willing to give. If we only focus on what we are going to get, nothing will grow. If the seed says, "I'm not going to give myself to the earth," it will never become a gardenia bush.

A mundane example of sacrifice is the gasoline in a car. It has to burn – it has to be sacrificed – in order for the car to move. If we try to preserve our tank of gas, we will never get anywhere.

A friend of mine served on the steering committee of her neighborhood association. She worked hard, volunteering many hours weekly for over two years. During this time, she often felt that other committee members didn't pull their weight. They weren't contributing and they didn't want to resign. They liked having their pictures posted at the clubhouse under the label, "Community Leaders."

My friend hinted many times that perhaps it was time for them to step down. If they left, there would be room for new people who might have more time to devote to the committee. No luck. Finally, in frustration, she resigned. And when she did, all the work fell to the remaining steering committee members. Without her carrying the majority of the load, they soon tendered their resignations.

Six months later, the new steering committee was introduced to the community. There was a big celebration to welcome the new and thank the old members. I watched as my friend sat in the back row, alone, while her cohorts received outgoing gifts. She had resigned months earlier, so she was not officially part of the "outgoing" committee and was not thanked publicly.

She was deeply hurt until someone pointed out to her the principle of sacrifice. In a way, she was the sacrificial lamb. If she hadn't resigned, the committee would never have changed. Returning to the example of an automobile, if we don't sacrifice the gasoline, the car doesn't move. My friend's sacrifice made it possible for her neighborhood committee to move on.

To Understand Sacrifice, Study Nature

The sun always rises. Does it ever say, "I've had it?" Never! Does it say, "I worked last week so I 'm going to relax?" No. It continues doing its duty. Can we perform our work, our service to the world, as selflessly as the elements perform their work for us?

Can we sacrifice our time? Perhaps we see others struggling to do a job that we know how to do. In the past, we may have struggled with the same issue or situation. We can take the time to help them. We can offer our expertise in how to make the most of time and resources. We can help them to organize their work because we've been through it. People appreciate this. When volunteers feel burdened or overwhelmed, telling them, "I will help you," eases the burden. Often, just the promise that help is on its way is enough to free them from pressure. When the burden is lifted, they often find their own solution.

Show that You Care

Everyone needs to feel supported and volunteers look to their leaders for sustenance and direction. There are innumerable ways to do this. For example:

1. Let people express their feelings. This simple gesture of support can relieve pressure and often frees up new energy. We can allow volunteers to voice their thoughts about how they feel without trying to "fix" them, or show them the errors of their ways.

2. Make things physically easier for the volunteers. Take care of their basic needs. If they are working in a room that is too crowded, do whatever needs to be done to create more space for them. Find ways to make the office or work area supportive and pleasant.

3. If someone is doing a great job on outdated equipment, try to get new equipment.

4. Ask, "Have you had lunch? Are you getting enough exercise? Sleep? Fresh air?"

5. Through your actions let volunteers know that you care.

You are Making the World Sacred

People who do volunteer work instinctively understand sacrifice. They may not be able to explain it, but they are in tune with this great principle. They give of themselves and through their sacrifice they are making the world sacred.

At the Robert B. McKay Community Outreach Law Program in New York City, many of the volunteer lawyers are activists who went into law to help the world. Along the way, they became successful in their profession. *Pro bono* volunteer work allows them to do what they originally set out to do.

Regularly the volunteer lawyers show up at the Legal Clinic for the Homeless to offer their services. The office is hot, stuffy, and cramped. The lawyers work hard and often for clients who disregard appointments or hearings, or who go back out on the streets and commit another crime, or who return to abusive spouses rather than follow through with legal action. In other words, the lawyers receive little thanks for what they offer. But they continue to serve.

Another example of real sacrifice is a woman who has recruited over 100 foster families in the state of Hawaii. This woman takes the sickest children into her own home. The children are often on respirators and need constant medical attention. Some of them cry continuously. They require enormous amounts of care.

How does she find homes for them? "God already knows where each child belongs," she says. "We just have to take care of them until the right family unit comes along."

As leaders, we can learn from these volunteers. Like the lawyers, we can continue to serve even if our efforts are not appreciated. Like the foster mother, we can do more than we ask others to do.

Because the earth thrives on sacrifice, the more selfless we become in our own work, the more our organization will prosper. Of course, some people interpret selfless as meaning that they don't take care of themselves—they give to the point of exhaustion. That is not true sacrifice and does not help the organization. Selflessness means giving without expecting to get in return. It is giving with detachment and without pride.

How to Inspire Cooperation

A leader who thinks and acts as an equal with the volunteers, who shares in the ups and the downs, inspires cooperation. When resources or volunteers are limited, *To Lead Is To Serve* means apply restrictions to yourself first.

Once, I volunteered for an organization with an executive director who redecorated his office during a hiring freeze. The volunteers were asked to take on more work to make up for the lack of staff, but when we saw his plush new digs none of us wanted to. When leaders don't apply restraints on themselves, they lose the respect of their associates. On the other hand, when they join in the sacrifice, they gain admiration.

During times of scarcity, by giving as much of yourself as you ask others to give of themselves, your work will be an inspiration and an example, which will attract followers. This is especially true if you manage to accomplish something in the lean times, which undoubtedly you will. During times when resources and volunteers are abundant, continue to apply restrictions to yourself. People will remember this. When the lean times come again, they will be more willing to cooperate and there will be no resentments

Sometimes we have to sacrifice our reputation for being a nice person. A leader is like the captain on a grand cruise ship. He dresses in his ocean whites and greets people graciously, mingling and chatting like the host at a dinner party. However, when there is a leak in the bow, instantly he is down the hatch plugging the holes or on the deck barking commands.

Some organizations have leaders who like being the captain hosting the party. They love the idea of hobnobbing in their nice clothes while the ship glides through calm waters. But when the seas get choppy, the ship runs aground because they don't want to get their whites dirty. They abandon their duty.

I volunteered at a food bank with a woman who was so enthusiastic and full of life that some people volunteered there just because she was so much fun. Quickly, she became a group leader, then an officer of the entire organization. Most of the volunteers were happy to see her rise through the ranks.

As time went by, she assumed more and more responsibility within the organization. Still, she wanted to remain every volunteer's best friend, so when someone did a poor job, she wouldn't say anything. In the name of being a nice person, she let the organization sink.

Organizations are also run aground by gossip, unrest, and dissatisfaction. These are like leaks in a ship. When they begin, how can the leader best serve? Not by retiring to the stateroom and refusing to become involved. The fear of being disliked is not an option for a leader. If gossip, for example, is affecting morale, stop it as immediately as a captain would plug holes in a ship. If there is dissatisfaction in the organization, instantly find out what the problem is and address it. Focus on getting the organization back on course by holding the original goal in mind.

When you look for the root of the problem, there is always the danger of finding out that the problem is you. If this happens, you may have to sacrifice some pride. Try to remember why you loved this organization in the first place then put your heart on your sleeve, apologize, and ask for permission to start over. If this happens to you, it will hurt. But you will come out a far stronger and better leader.

If, instead, you choose to sacrifice the organization to save your reputation, you'll lose your reputation regardless.

Become Great

When we sacrifice, we open a space for something more valuable to emerge. The challenges that arise and call for sacrifice are occasions to develop into a greater human being. If you accept the challenge, you will be given an opportunity to offer your strength, knowledge, and experience to your organization and to your volunteers.

Only the seeds that offer themselves to the earth become trees. In the same way, only leaders who sacrifice have the opportunity to become great.

GEMS to
REMEMBER
℘

1
When something is given up, it makes
room for something else to evolve.
The neighborhood association.

2
Serve like nature serves.
Making things easier for others.

3
Continue to serve even when
unappreciated.
The New York City volunteer lawyers.

4
Do more than you ask of others.
The foster mother.

5
Sacrifice your popularity.
The captain on the cruise ship.

6
In the name of being nice, are you
letting your organization sink?
The woman at the food bank.

7
Only leaders who sacrifice
earn the opportunity
to become great.
Seeds sacrifice themselves to become trees.

EXERCISE
for SUCCESS

1
Think of a time when someone wanted
something from you and you felt that you
were too busy to give it. Write down
what happened.

2
What could have happened if you had been
willing to sacrifice your time to help?

3
Look over a list of people who work with
you. Who needs more from you? How
can you serve these people?

5

Listen!

.. want to be heard, understood, loved...

to listen is to learn

Listening is an Investment

℘

CHAPTER FIVE

One way to judge

our effectiveness

as a leader is

by the amount

of honest feedback

that we get.

John F. Kennedy

℘

The fifth step is to listen.

Taking the time to listen to people can be your greatest contribution. Listening is a way of showing appreciation. If you listen to people first, they will be able to hear you when it is your turn to speak.

T.C. Yim was a state senator in Hawaii for many years. Later he was Executive Director of the Office of Hawaiian Affairs. One day an angry staffer came into his office and began to rant. He complained for more than 30 minutes. Yim didn't say a word. He just listened as the man poured out his grievance. When the man finished, Yim said, "It's noon. Would you like to have lunch?" They finished the conversation over a meal and the man became one of the senator's best employees.

Yim, like all leaders, is action-oriented. His first impulse, in the midst of a busy morning with a full calendar, was to cut the staffer off and try to change his mind or set him straight. Instead, he listened and salvaged the relationship with a good employee.

To stop and listen appears to halt the momentum of our work. But does it? In Yim's case, it kept the momentum flowing.

People want to be listened to. We all want to be heard. Isn't this why focus groups are so popular? One organization sent invitations out that read, "We want your input so come and help us plan our goals for the next five years." More than 900 people responded! So many people came that the event had to be moved to a hotel ballroom.

Imagine if the organizers had sent an invitation that read, "We want to tell you what we are planning to do for the next five years. Please come." How many people would have responded? Perhaps only a handful.

No matter how busy we are, we can find the time to listen. In a crisis, we must make time to listen on the spot, just as the senator did. At less critical moments, we can make appointments to listen later.

There are situations when it is especially beneficial to listen. For example, before you begin a new project and after the project is completed. If you will take the time to listen to everyone's ideas at the beginning, it will pay off in the long run. Those who offer their thoughts will have a sense of ownership of the project and will contribute as stakeholders.

Then, when the project is completed, listen to everyone's comments and praise their good work. Volunteers enjoy ruminating about a job well done. Honor their sense of accomplishment by listening to them.

By making it a point to listen at the beginning and end of a project, you gain an overview of the work.

Listen and Learn

One more good reason to listen: To learn. Sometimes it is difficult to listen to people who disagree with us or who don't share our point of view. But if we are open to suggestions our organization will benefit.

The Children's Hope Foundation helps children with AIDS. The organization is young and growing fast. To make sure it stays on track, the board of directors meets regularly with volunteers, doctors, and social workers to simply ask, "What can we do better?" The organization has prospered from the advice it has received.

In the same way, not taking the time to listen can cause you to miss valuable opportunities. In Philadelphia, a volunteer for a non-profit went to work for a printing company. In her new job, she saw that she could save her volunteer organization a lot of money on printing. She called the person in charge of the organization's publications and offered a significant saving on the printing of its newsletter. The person never returned her call. The volunteer tried again. No response, again. It seems the person in charge of printing was too busy to listen and learn about a nice offer.

Listening well can save valuable time and give us information about people – about what they know and what they need to know. When we assume we already know – when we don't listen – the time we waste could be our own.

Master chef Deborah DeWitt was teaching a gourmet cooking class to a group of young businessmen. Because the class was taught at an upscale cookware store and had been advertised as gourmet, the chef assumed that her students were experienced cooks. Wrong.

Two-thirds of the way through the class one young man asked, "Why do you keep talking about stock? Why would stocks and bonds have anything to do with cooking?"

Deborah said, "Oh, dear! Back to basics."

The moral is: Know your audience. Never assume that people understand you. This man spent most of the class confused. Of course, after he asked his question the instructor did clarify and inform the young stockbroker about the culinary stocks. Now she takes time at the beginning of her classes to listen to the students and learn about them.

An Investment That Pays Dividends

If we do not listen to volunteers, they will think we do not value them. We do, so we must listen. At an organization where I volunteer, I was asked to help brainstorm ideas for a special celebration. Over a two-day period, a group of us spent eight hours coming up with creative ideas for the event. Excited, we went back to the organizers to present our thoughts.

When we arrived for our meeting, the person in charge announced, "Here's the plan. This is what we are doing." While we had been brainstorming, the organizers had come up with their own plan and had already begun to implement it.

It was a painful moment. I had been thrilled to be invited to the brainstorming session. I was happy to sit in all the meetings. But I was deeply hurt that our ideas were not even listened to. We knew that our suggestions might not be accepted, but we thought we would be able to present them.

Volunteers feel dejected when the opportunity to serve is taken away from them. That was how I felt that day – dejected. The upside was that it made me reflect on all the times that I had done the same thing to others. I truly regret those instances when I turned people away who wanted to help because I didn't take the time to listen to them.

We cannot expect people to invest energy in our organization unless we are willing to invest time in them. Listening is an investment. It is the single most important thing we can do to let volunteers know we value and respect them. When we listen to others, and really hear them, they often respond in amazing ways.

When I first became a journalist I was surprised and a bit confused by the number of men whom I interviewed who became infatuated with me. Some professed they were falling in love. These men knew nothing about me and I did not understand why it was happening. Finally, it dawned on me that it was because I was listening to them. Listening communicates caring. All people love it.

To become an effective listener, we have to stop talking and, just as important, stop thinking about what we wish to express. How often do we miss what the other person is saying because we are busy planning what we are going to say next?

Listening is an investment that pays enormous dividends.

Why Volunteers Quit

The number one reason why volunteers quit is hurt feelings. For this reason, when a volunteer expresses that his feelings are hurt, take time to listen. Go for a walk together and remember *To Lead Is To Serve.* Concentrate on understanding how he feels. Listen for what is really being expressed. Often it is hurt pride. Even if you think he is being ridiculous, just listen. Don't offer solutions. When a person is drowning is not the time to give swimming instructions. Similarly, when feelings are hurt is not the time to teach a lesson. We can throw a lifeline by listening.

The last thing you need to do when someone has made a big mistake is to say, "I told you so." No matter how good your advice is, the person will not hear it while he is upset. Hold back and say something sympathetic such as," I know this meant a lot to you," or "It must feel awful to work so hard and not have it go as you expected."

Holding back is one of the most difficult things for a leader to do. Real leaders see solutions easily. They see what went wrong and how it can be fixed. The impulse to speak up is strong. However, when someone has just blown it is not the time to start analyzing the situation. It is the time, instead, to put your brakes on and exercise patience.

According to ancient Chinese wisdom, patience in the highest sense means "putting brakes on strength." Hold back your opinion and simply listen. Then sympathize. Even if a volunteer is completely in the wrong. Even if the upset is due to her own anger or stubbornness. To keep an employee, a volunteer, or a friend – listen.

GEMS *to* REMEMBER

℘

1
Taking time to listen to people can be our greatest contribution.
The senator and the angry staffer.

2
People want to be listened to.
900 people wanting to offer ideas.

3
Be _open_ to suggestions.
The discounted printing offer.

4
Listening makes people feel valued.
The brainstorming session.

5
The number one reason volunteers quit.
Hurt feelings.

6
Know your audience.
The cooking class.

7
Hold back your opinion and simply listen.
Patience means putting brakes on strength.

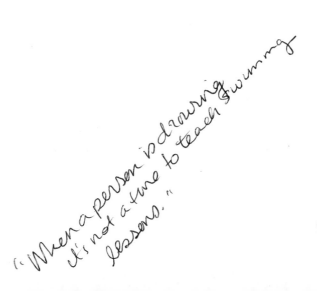

"When a person is drowning it's not a time to teach swimming lessons."

EXERCISE
for SUCCESS

1

Schedule time to visit every department to listen and give your support. The department you resist visiting probably needs you the most.

2

Create a list of people to call. You may be on the telephone so much that making another call seems ghastly, but there are volunteers who would love to receive a call from you. Include even the most modest people who faithfully perform the tasks that the organization depends on.

3

Make the calls and find out what each person is thinking. Catch yourself if you find that you are talking more than listening.

6

Inspiring, Informative Meetings

℘

CHAPTER SIX

When all is
said and done,
more is said
than done.

Italian Proverb

ℰ

The sixth step is to run inspiring,
informative meetings.

Good meetings are essential to your organization's success. Inspiring, informative meetings keep volunteers coming back. Boring meetings cause volunteers to resign. Successful, brief meetings will strengthen your volunteer force and your organization.

One of the most important things to remember about meetings is this: when you talk too much, on a subtle level people begin to dislike you.

Look at it like serving tea to your volunteers. How do people feel when we offer them a cup of tea? As we begin to pour, they feel nourished and grateful, don't they? But what happens when the tea reaches the rim of the cup? Their feelings begin to change. They get anxious. If we continue pouring, the tea spills over the rim into the saucer and onto their hands, clothes, shoes, and the floor.

How do they feel now?

It is exactly the same when we talk too much at a meeting. A little is wonderful. A lot is dreadful. Remember: *To Lead Is To Serve.* We want to give information that serves the volunteers. We do not want to overwhelm them with information overload. Or, worse, bore them.

Use meetings to inspire, evaluate current projects, follow-through, inform, train. Do not use meetings to bore, blame or discourage.

Before You Begin

Set the Goal

Begin the meeting by saying, "The purpose of this meeting is..."

Plan the Agenda

An old saying goes, *"When all is said and done, more is said than done."* Do not let this happen. The person in charge has to structure the meeting with clear agenda points. Then she must make sure that the agenda is covered and that action points are recorded.

Once, I served on a committee where the chairwoman opened every weekly meeting with, "OK. What do we have to do this week?" She never took time to prepare an agenda. It is amazing how many people expect us to spend more of our time listening to them than they have spent in preparing their comments.

Respect Time

Almost every successful person I interviewed for this book commented on the importance of respecting people's time. Start at the appointed hour. Do not go overtime. Do not ramble.

Five Keys To Running a Successful Meeting

1. Be Inspiring

The word "inspire" means to take an in-breath, which brings energy into the body. We cannot do anything if we cannot breathe. To inspire others, we first have to inspire ourselves. To be fascinating, we must fascinate ourselves first. Only after we are inspired through our enthusiasm, confidence, and goodwill will we be able to inspire others.

Here are some suggestions for how to inspire yourself and others at every meeting:

- Share your favorite experiences of volunteering.
- Read a quote giving hope.
- Tell an uplifting story.
- Announce news that is exciting to the group, i.e. "We just got a big contract or donation," or "A TV station mentioned our project on the news."
- Read a thank-you letter.

2. Follow-Through

Briefly mention an action point from the last meeting and how it has been applied or completed. Following through tells people that their time at the last meeting was well spent. A brief follow-through is best because it emphasizes action points and keeps important material in view without repeating it in detail.

Follow-through is an excellent way to keep the mission of the organization alive in the hearts and minds of volunteers. Successful organizations have clear, understandable mission statements and they keep revisiting them. An important aspect of follow-through is to relate current projects to the overall goals of the organization.

3. Inform

Give information liberally and generously. Volunteers like to be informed, especially about anything that has to do with their own work. They love statistics about themselves and their work.

Announce, "This year we have contacted over 6,100 new people; sent out 25,000 pieces of mail; eaten 367 cheese sandwiches, etc."

Use meetings to tell what has happened since the last meeting and what events and projects are coming up. Organizations I have observed that keep information within a small group, end up being small organizations. Make it a point to inform everyone who needs to be informed and err on the side of too many rather than too few. When the executive director is going to an important conference, tell people where he is going. This makes individuals feel included and keeps them interested and invested in the work.

One nationwide service organization had an entire department of staff and volunteers quit. Why? Every day the administrator went off to the legislature saying that she was going "to lobby." Nothing was explained. The staff and volunteers felt left out, so they quit.

Human beings are always striving for union. We are social animals and this desire to be a part of a greater whole is powerful. When we feel included, we give our support. When we feel excluded, we may try to undermine those we feel are excluding us. Use meetings to share information and to build a strong team in which everyone feels included.

The Metropolitan Museum of Art in New York City has 1,700 employees and 700 volunteers. Together they make a fantastic team. The museum's Vice President of Development told me, "The volunteers are involved in everything. Giving the volunteers the feeling of belonging is a core function of the museum. They receive the staff newsletter and the volunteer chairperson attends the meetings of the board of trustees."

Another benefit of sharing information freely is that your organization will get free publicity. Word of mouth is the most effective form of advertising. Build enthusiasm for a project by announcing, "A great event is taking place." Your volunteers will spread the word for you.

Public relations expert Dr. Helen Varner says, "An employee on the bus is more important to you than a P.R. person on the evening news. Regularly make sure everyone in the organization knows what is going on."

4. Evaluate

The definition of evaluate is "to determine the value of." When we move on to the next project without evaluating the last one, we may not appreciate what we have done. We may miss out on the gems of what we have accomplished. Take time to evaluate what went right and what went wrong on every project.

First, ask everyone in the meeting to write down their delights and concerns, plus solutions to any challenges that came up during the project. Don't give your thoughts first. Let others share their thoughts, then have a discussion based on some simple questions:

• What worked really well?

- How can we improve next time? No matter how good it was, we want to make it better.
- What can we do together to improve?
- What could each of us do individually?
- What did you learn from the work?
- What will you do differently next time?

Everyone remembers what they say more than what you tell them. If they verbalize what they have learned, they will not forget it and they will be stronger for the next project.

We all have great experiences doing volunteer work. Verbalizing these experiences keeps us inspired. If we have a bad experience, verbalizing it gets it off our chest so that we can move on.

Pay attention and learn from evaluations.

5. Train and Educate

Once, I volunteered for an organization that regularly had large in-house trainings for the entire staff of volunteers. The trainings not only advanced the work of the organization, but also enhanced the lives of the volunteers by giving them tools that they could use away from their work as volunteers. These trainings created enthusiasm that kept volunteers committed to the organization.

Make time in regular meetings for in-house trainings. First do business, then have a session in which volunteers learn skills and receive information that they can use. The more closely the training is tied to a current project the better.

Some in-house training ideas:
- Using the telephone
- Listening
- How to talk about the organization
- How to write a press release

Volunteers are eager to learn, so take advantage of opportunities to expand their knowledge. If your organization can afford to send people to outside trainings, then do it. The investment will pay off.

Two women went to work as development directors for two different organizations. One was a school, the other a city zoo. Neither woman had experience in professional fundraising. The first one received extensive training and was sent to a myriad of seminars. The other was expected to learn on the job. Her organization claimed that it did not have time or funds for "frills" like trainings. Within three months, donations began flowing in for one organization. Can you guess which one?

Teleclasses are an excellent, affordable way to train your staff and volunteers. Taught by telephone conference call, participants receive personal instruction without having to travel or take a whole day out of the office. You can find out more about "Learn by Phone" training teleclasses at the *To Lead Is To Serve* website: www.toleadistoserve.com.

For advice on fundraising, visit my website www.JoyofLeadership.com

GEMS to
REMEMBER
℘

1
Before you begin: set a goal, plan the agenda and respect time.
Chairperson who opened meetings with, "What do we do this week?

2
If you talk too much, on a subtle level people begin to dislike you.
Overflowing teacup.

3
Inspiration creates energy.
Fascinate yourself first.

4
Word of mouth is the most effective form of advertising.
The employee on the bus.

5

Successful organizations have clear,
understandable missions.
*Follow-through by relating
current projects to overall goals.*

6

. Human beings strive for union.
The Metropolitan Museum of Art.

7

People love learning and your
organization benefits.
The two new fundraisers.

EXERCISE
for SUCCESS

Plan a meeting using these steps:

1
Define the purpose of the meeting.

2
How will you inspire people? What story
or quote will be shared?
Who could tell the story?

3
On which subjects will you follow-through
from the last meeting?

4
What new information will you
and others offer?

5
Which projects need to be evaluated
at the meeting?

6
Will you include training in this meeting?
If so, on what subject?

7
What time will the meeting
begin and end?

7

Be Attractive

ℒ

CHAPTER SEVEN

Cleanliness and order

are not matters

of instinct;

they are matters of education,

and like most great things,

you must cultivate

a taste for them.

Benjamin Disraeli

℘

The seventh step is to be attractive.

Jerry Van Camp is a pilot who was the chairman of his pilots' union. The union meetings were held in a room where everyone smoked, ate, and drank coffee. Subsequently, it was a mess. At one point, the union was negotiating a new contract and the two sides were stuck in a deadlock. Many meetings had taken place without reaching an agreement.

One night, before a crucial meeting, Jerry went into that room and cleaned the whole area himself. He vacuumed, dusted, and rearranged the chairs. The chairman became the servant, and the next morning the energy in the room had shifted. The air was clear. It felt good to be in that room. Fresh thoughts seemed to spring forth from the atmosphere and the negotiators discovered a perfect solution.

The law of attraction is not a technique. It is a natural phenomenon.

If your organization is having trouble with recruiting volunteers ask yourself, "How am I feeling about my own work? Am I attracted to what I am doing? If not, how will I possibly attract others?"

To attract volunteers, become attractive.

Does this mean going to a plastic surgeon for a facelift? No. It is much deeper than that. The true power of attraction is based on visible and invisible factors. As an example, think of a coffee cup. When we want to put fresh coffee into a cup, we first pour out the old coffee. No one wants to drink a cup full of old coffee grounds.

To become an attractive organization, clear out negativities, which are like the dregs of the cup. Like washing out the old coffee grounds, clear away secret resentments, jealousies, and attitudes that interfere with the work and prevent the organization from fulfilling its potential.

Don't Worry

Worry is a negativity that repels volunteers. Have you noticed that when you feel overwhelmed or worried, no one volunteers? On the other hand, when you are feeling positive about your work, others are attracted and want to join your cause.

A magnet has two poles. The positive side attracts and the negative side repels. A great leader who is capable of attracting people to join in will always identify with the positive.

At the height of World War II when he was working 18 hours a day, Winston Churchill was asked if he worried about his tremendous responsibilities. He replied, "I am too busy. I have no time for worry."

If you are worried about how to *get* volunteers, you can turn the situation around by asking, "What do I need to give?"

There is a businessman in Australia who turned his enterprise around this way. When a recession hit, he found himself facing severe financial difficulties. Not knowing what to do, he went to an advisor and asked for help. He was expecting suggestions such as, "Sell this or that. Lay off employees. Cut back."

Instead, he was given some interesting advice. He was told, "Treat all of your employees as brothers and sisters. You cannot get your business together externally until you get it together internally."

Failure
is the
opportunity
to begin again
more
intelligently

Henry Ford

Based on the advice he received, the Australian businessman changed his focus. Instead of only looking at the bottom line, he started looking at what he could give to his employees. He saw that they needed better working conditions and better benefits. He went through every level of the firm and looked at each person's situation. He asked himself, "How would I treat them if they were my brothers and sisters?"

With this criterion, he made a plan. It would cost money to do the things he needed to do, so he reluctantly sold his beautiful mansion to raise cash. Then he asked for the support of the employees. He rallied them, saying, "Look, we are in a tough situation," but he tried to save every job. He did everything he could, treating each employee like a brother or a sister.

This businessman's actions attracted the loyalty and commitment of the employees. They worked hard and as a team went through the company's challenges. It is a classic example of a leader serving the people who, in turn, gave him their full support. The business turned around and now his products are sold in many parts of the world, including the United States, Hong Kong, and Japan. It turned out that he sold his house at the top of the market, right before a drop in the price of real estate. Later, he easily bought another.

Openness and Cleanliness are Attractive

Resources that are not circulated freely tend to congest the whole system. Is there an area of your office that is off-limits to everyone except management? Or does management get some perks that could be opened up to everyone? Excluding people creates animosity and jealousy. Everything can stagnate from one paltry thing that is hoarded. When resources flow freely, everyone feels they are part of the whole. A free flow of resources changes attitudes and creates a feeling like fresh air within the organization.

If the doors of perception were cleansed, everything would appear as it is —
infinite.

William Blake

There is everything to be said for an attractive office. Cleanliness and neatness say a lot about an organization and the people who work and volunteer there. Clutter and old stuff hidden in closets and desk drawers drags down the energy, keeping it from flowing properly. When an office is neat and clean with flowers and furniture arranged in a nice way, it will attract both good volunteers and good ideas.

Just think about it: if we are going to have guests for dinner in our home, we clean house beforehand. We can do the same thing at the office. To attract good volunteers, clean the workspace and make it attractive.

When We Take Good Care of What We Have, More Comes to Us

I knew an industrious woman who worked for a worldwide organization writing its newsletter. She had to travel in her work and for the first two years she used an old manual typewriter that she set up on her hotel room bed. She treated that typewriter like a great friend. With it, she put out an excellent newsletter. Of course, her talent and her attitude of respect for the tool of her trade, modest though it was, came to the attention of the company executives. Later, she was promoted again and again and soon she was travelling with a staff and all the computer support that she needed.

Another woman, who was about the same age and equally as bright, joined the organization at the same time. She made many demands, saying that her job could not be done unless she was given better equipment and more help. What do you think happened to that woman? Nothing. Her career came to a screeching halt in that organization.

This doesn't mean that people who ask for better equipment are bad employees or volunteers. It means that attitude is important. Appreciating and caring for what we do have and using it to the best of our ability opens us to receive more.

Nature fills up things that are empty and tears down what is full. Valleys are filled in and mountains are worn down. When the moon is full, it begins to wane and when it is dark, it waxes again. This happens in the lives of people, too. We hate the proud and love the modest.

When a person holds a high position
and is nevertheless modest,
he shines with the light of wisdom;
if he is in a lowly position
and is modest,
he cannot be passed by.

I Ching

When we honor what we have, more comes to us. In front of the Plaza Hotel in New York City there is a famous statue. A few years ago it had fallen into disrepair. It was dirty and uncared for. One day, attorney Ira Millstein looked out of his office window across the street and had an idea that prompted him to create what he called the "voluntary window tax." All the offices with windows facing the statue were asked to pay it. Millstein raised $4 million, enough money to fix the statue and put some in trust to keep it clean and in good repair. Later, it was learned that the statue is the image of a Greek goddess whose promise is that whoever treats her with respect will be rewarded.

In Oakland, California, a neighborhood conducted a clean-up campaign that included planting trees along Stanford Avenue and creating a small park. After all the cleaning up, residents discovered that the neighborhood's crime rate had diminished.

When we take good care of what we have, we will attract more.

Enthusiasm Attracts Volunteers

There is an elderly Hawaiian woman who has attracted many volunteers for the Queen Emma Museum in Honolulu. When I asked her where she finds these volunteers, she said, "At the supermarket."

Can you imagine a lady with gray hair wearing a muumuu and flower garland standing in line at the checkout counter asking someone to volunteer? I couldn't, so I asked, "The supermarket?"

She responded, "Well, the supermarket and everywhere else, too. I just love to volunteer, so I can't stop talking about it."

Enthusiasm is extremely attractive. What is wonderful about volunteering? What is irresistible about our organization? Enthusiastically sharing that with others so that they feel it, too, is true public relations.

The word *enthusiasm* means, "filled with God" and *to attract* means, "to offer pleasure and delight." We offer pleasure when we talk about the sizzle of our organization. The sizzle of attraction works like a magnet – it draws others and keeps them coming back.

The key to truly attracting people lies in the definition of "attract." It means "to offer pleasure and delight." When you are absolutely delighted, you will attract volunteers.

Let Time Take Care of It

After you have given your best efforts to clean up your organization internally and externally, be patient. Sooner or later volunteers will be attracted. They *will* come. If they do not come immediately, don't worry.

The struggle to get out of the cocoon is exactly what makes a butterfly strong enough to fly. If we open a cocoon too soon, the butterfly dies. If we are willing to wait, in its own time the butterfly can take flight.

In the same way, if your efforts do not attract volunteers right away, don't feel devastated. Just wait and let time take care of it.

GEMS to
REMEMBER
℘

1
To attract volunteers, become attractive.
The airline pilots' meeting place.

2
Clear out negativities.
Winston Churchill during World War II.

3
Treat staff and volunteers like brothers
and sisters.
The Australian businessman.

4
Resources that are not circulated freely
congest the whole system.
Hording possessions.

5
When we take good care of what we have,
more comes to us.
The newsletter editor.

6
Enthusiasm is attractive.
The volunteer at the Queen Emma Museum.

7
If your efforts do not attract volunteers
right away, give it time.
The butterfly.

EXERCISE *for* SUCCESS

1

What is keeping your organization from being attractive? How could each challenge be eliminated using *To Lead Is To Serve?*

2

Is the office clean and uncluttered? Are there storage areas that can be culled? When was the last time that the office files were updated? Make a checklist for daily and weekly cleaning. Once a month, set aside half a day for everyone to clean their desks and work areas and to update files. This will attract new volunteers and donors.

3

What delights you about your organization? Tell five people.

8

Change Your Mind

As we think,

so we become.

Upanishads

℘

The eighth step is to change your mind.

A woman in a café left her table for a few moments and returned to discover a beggar eating her meal. She sat down, glaring at him while he ate her lunch. She was furious until he offered to share his cup of tea. Surprised, she accepted the tea and began to change her mind about him.

Then she noticed that the bag of groceries she had left on the chair at her table was missing. Immediately she changed her mind again.

"This beggar is nothing but a thief," she fumed.

Eventually the beggar finished the meal and rose to leave. When he left his seat, the woman could see past him to the next table. She saw that in the chair was her bag of groceries and on the table was her meal. Earlier, when she had come back to her seat, she had returned to the wrong table. She had created the whole incident in her own mind!

The Upanishads say, "As we think, so we become." If we think something is delightful, it is delightful. If we think it is going to be overwhelming, there's a good chance that it will be. The woman in the café thought that the man was eating her meal. The moment she had that thought, she experienced all the upset that the situation would induce if it were true – even though it wasn't.

The mind is analogous to an empty glass. Whatever we fill the glass with, it becomes that. If we fill it with dirty water, it becomes dirty. If we add salt, it becomes salty. If we pour champagne into the glass, it becomes bubbly. Similarly, if we fill the mind with a powerful, constructive thought, that becomes our experience.

Think and Become Great

The mind can create any situation. When we are in charge, we have the opportunity to create the situation we desire. We can create an atmosphere that attracts people like bees to honey or we can drive them away. It is our choice, always. What we choose to think and to focus on determines the outcome of any situation. It is especially important to remember this when the chips are down. Any leader can shine when his team is winning. It takes an outstanding leader to inspire volunteers to climb an uphill path.

Abraham Lincoln was a true leader. As president of the United States during the Civil War, he stirred the hearts and minds of Americans with his words and his conviction in what he saw as the highest Truth. When the North was fighting against the South and families were fighting against each other, nothing could sway Lincoln from his fundamental beliefs. At Gettysburg he said: "Four score and seven years ago our fathers brought forth upon this continent a new nation, conceived in liberty, and dedicated to the proposition that all men are created equal."

How was Lincoln able to speak such inspiring words in the midst of one of the darkest moments in history? He was able to change his own mind. He did not let the situation become discouraging. He lived the principle of *To Lead Is To Serve* and turned to his highest ideals to inspire himself and his troops.

As a young man, Abraham Lincoln received less than one year of formal education. He spent his childhood working on a farm. While he was plowing the fields he memorized Aesop's fables. The moral of one of the fables is, "A house divided against itself cannot stand." Lincoln filled his mind with this wisdom. Years later, during the crisis between the states, Lincoln declared, "A nation divided against itself cannot stand." Lincoln used the wisdom he imbibed as a youth to save the union.

Our attitude makes the difference. It determines whether the group feels a situation is difficult or that it is challenging and worthwhile. How many times have we heard the leader say, "We have so much work and we don't have enough volunteers. What are we going to do?" (Perhaps we have been the leader saying this.) If the leader chooses this point of view, what will everyone else think?

This does not mean that when we are feeling discouraged that we stand up and say, "Everything is rosy." Never! People know when they are being lied to. When we feel bleak, we can turn to what inspires us about the work. We can change our own mind before we spread our discouragement to others.

The challenge to the leader is to remain focussed on what is great and inspiring about the project. As part of the planning process, at the very beginning, we can ask ourselves, "Why am I doing this in the first place?" Then we can go back to this intention throughout the project.

At any moment, the mind can pull us up or take us down. The attitude in the mind of the leader affects the whole group, so we have to be careful.

The World Is As You See It

Two people can see the same situation in completely different ways based on the way each one views the world.

Several years ago, Dr. Hal Ferrar was standing in a long line at a bank in Manhattan. He could see that he would be there for awhile, so he decided to make the best of it. He began whistling a happy tune.

Standing in front of him was a lady who was gray all over, from her coat to her hat, including the gray cloud of smoke circling above her cigarette.

She was mumbling to herself, obviously disgruntled about having to wait in the long line. Dr. Ferrar continued to whistle.

Suddenly, the gray lady whirled around and shouted, "What are you whistling about?"

Taken aback, he replied,

"I'm just happy, I guess."

Then the lady asked,

"Do you want to know why you are happy?"

"Why?" he inquired.

"Because God is so busy torturing me that He doesn't have time for you!" she growled.

We cook in our own sauce.

Spanish Proverb

How to Change Your Own Mind

Our thoughts really do create our experiences. A little negativity so quickly becomes a demon, a mental monster. On the other hand, a smile can turn a negative situation around.

I once read a tip for driving that said if you rear-end someone (which hopefully you won't), get out of the car with a big smile on your face. Say, "Gee, I didn't mean to do that. I am very sorry." Keep smiling and it will be difficult for the other driver to be mad.

I suggested that a friend mention this in a lecture that he was preparing. He didn't want to because he did not believe it. Then, the next day he and a passenger were driving down the street. They passed a maternity shop that had a nude, pregnant mannequin in the window. The passenger laughed and said, "Look!" As my friend turned to look, he rear-ended the car ahead of him. It was a big, shiny, black truck. The driver of the truck looked like a body builder as he angrily leapt from behind the wheel.

My friend froze. Then he remembered the story and put on a big smile, saying, "Gee, I didn't mean to do that. I'm very sorry."

The body builder became mild as a lamb. He said, "There's no damage. Don't do it again," and drove off.

My friend happily included the driving tip in his lecture.

Human beings can alter their lives
by altering their attitudes of mind.

William James

How do we alter our attitudes of mind? How can we change our negative thoughts into positive ones? The most important thing we can do is to step back and watch. Witness your own mind. See how it works, how it chooses the negative or the positive. If we can watch our own thoughts without judging them, great positive growth and true self-acceptance begins.

Watching without judging is "witnessing." It creates detachment from painful experiences and it is the beginning of freedom from the negative tendencies of the mind. Zen masters teach the technique of "watching the train go by." We can watch our thoughts just like we watch the cars on a freight train. We can watch them go by but we do not have to jump on.

Witnessing your thoughts is very helpful when a volunteer is annoying you. Reacting or commenting on your annoyance is like jumping on the train. Instead, just watch your thoughts.

"Oh, I notice that I'm annoyed with Jane again," you might say to yourself. Or, "Bill upsets me with his disorganization. My irritation with Bill comes up often." When you begin watching your thoughts, you'll also see how quickly they go by.

Play it Again, Sam

In addition to watching the train go by, we can also change the movie in our mind. We can roll a new movie up on the screen and watch any scene play out in a better way. Film makers and recording artists do this all the time. When recording artists don't like the way a certain track sounds, they go back and record it again. But when we do something we don't like, we think that we're stuck with it. Often, we replay our mistakes over and over again in our mind.

By mentally repeating the bad scene, we increase the chances that it will occur again and that the outcome will be the same. By changing the scene mentally, we increase the likelihood that we'll do better next time.

How to Help Others Change Their Minds

It is not uncommon to hear a volunteer say, "When I first became a volunteer, it was so exciting, so rewarding. Then it became work; sometimes even drudgery."

To help a volunteer who feels burdened, have her go back to the beginning. Ask, "Why did you begin volunteering in the first place? What originally sparked your interest?" Chances are, that spark is still there, smoldering under the pressure. Uncover it and fan the flame of that original impulse.

Before we can help others, however, we must be sure that we are not feeling burdened ourselves.

It is like using an oxygen mask on an airplane: First we must be certain that we can breathe, then we can assist others.

Succeed with
Tom Sawyer's Style

When we are enthusiastic about our work, everyone wants to join in. When we feel burdened, we find ourselves wondering where everyone went. Remember Tom Sawyer painting the fence? When he thought of it as an unpleasant chore, no one wanted to help him. But when he changed his attitude and acted like his task was his greatest joy, people begged for a chance to paint the fence.

Holly Henderson, the coordinator of HELP for Non-Profits in Honolulu counsels, "When there are not enough resources to go around and the community psyche is depressed, being upbeat instead of tragic is very important."

Holly recommends adopting the Assets Planning Model, which looks at what resources an organization has before evaluating its needs. It starts with, "What are the strengths?" instead of "What is missing?" This method can be applied to individuals as well as to organizations.

For instance, if you have an employee who has gotten into trouble, instead of looking for his weaknesses, make a list of his assets: He has a good sense of self-image, he's great with people, he has done the job well for several years. Emphasize these assets as you work with him.

This approach is similar to an accountant researching investment opportunities. If a business has strong assets, it is a good investment. Likewise, people with strong assets are wonderful investments.

Holly says that by making it a habit to focus on strengths and possibilities first, we can identify assets and resources that we would otherwise overlook. In the long run this benefits our projects.

"If we focus on need, need, need, we are going to drown in depression and repel volunteers," she says. "But we will attract volunteers by focussing on the attributes of our organization. Then people will get involved because they think the organization can make an impact and that they can help. Be sure to give them a real chance to do that."

How to Make it Possible for People to Say Yes

How we say something makes a formidable difference. The story is told of two high school girls. One asked the gym teacher, "May I eat ice cream when I begin dieting?"

"Absolutely not!" said the teacher.

The other student then asked, "May I begin dieting while I eat ice cream?"

"Absolutely!"

The response we get depends on how we phrase our statement or question.

How does it feel when someone says, "Like it or not, we've got a big job to do?" Don't you imagine that a big struggle lies ahead? When I hear a comment like this, my energy drops. I get defensive.

On the other hand, what do we think when we hear, "I have some good news?" We sparkle. We lean forward in our chair. We want to hear it. The same holds true when someone says, "We have a challenge," as opposed to, "We have a problem."

A positive statement versus a negative one actually physically changes us inside. Human beings are physically attracted to people who use positive words. As the leader, we can serve the organization and the volunteers by changing our negative words into positive ones.

There is always a lot of laughter in seminars when we ask people to re-write their complaints using positive sentences. They think of a task that seems overwhelming, then they write three positive things about the task.

When journalist Kekoa Enomoto did this exercise she sighed, "I am overwhelmed by the things on my desk." So I asked her to write about the work on her desk in a positive way. She laughed and then wrote: "I love my mail! It gives me ideas. It makes me a better reporter because I'm on top of the news and therefore the earlier I get to the mail, the more on top of the news I'll be! March right through that mail!"

A Small Change Can Make a Big Difference

Gwen Jackson held the position of National Chairman of Volunteers for the American Red Cross from 1989 to 1991. When she arrived in Washington, D.C., the first thing she did was to change the name on the office door from "Office of the National Chairman of Volunteers" to "National Office of Volunteers." In addition to eliminating the gender reference, she made it the volunteers' office, not her office. This small change marked a tremendous shift in attitude in the organization.

Small ways of reorganizing our thinking can make an enormous difference. The more organized our thoughts are, the more confident we will feel and the more competent we will be perceived to be. Numbering points, for example, helps people to remember them. You can say, "I am going to give you three ideas today," or "This program has six steps." This brings clarity to the work, making it easy to understand for everyone.

Gwen Jackson says, "You help people remember when you conceptualize your formula." Her formula for volunteerism is:

Three C's & an A
Caring, Committed, Competent
& Accountable

As we think, so we become. Change your mind and watch yourself become a powerful, constructive volunteer leader.

GEMS to REMEMBER

1
The mind can create anything.
The woman and the beggar.

2
Fill your mind with powerful, constructive thoughts.
Abraham Lincoln.

3
People view the same situation in different ways.
The doctor and the gray lady in the bank.

4
To change your mind, witness your thoughts.
Watch the train go by.

5
To help others change their minds, focus on the fun.
Tom Sawyer painting the fence.

6
Positive words equal a positive response.
The gym teacher and the ice cream.

7
Small changes make a big difference.
The Red Cross Office of Volunteers.

EXERCISE
for SUCCESS

1

Ask yourself these questions:

What did you love about this job
at the beginning?
What was important about this work?
What is challenging about this job?
What is fun about it?
How is it worthwhile?

Write these questions on a 3" x 5" card
and then ask them to yourself every time
you feel burdened. The answers can rekindle
your enthusiasm.

2

Think about a challenging situation. Next,
watch all the thoughts you have about it as if
you were watching a movie. Sit back and roll
the thoughts up on the screen in your mind,
like rolling credits at the end of a film.

3

Recall an incident that did not go the way you wanted. Recall yourself in the situation. What you said. What you thought. What you did

4

Now re-write the script. Imagine it differently and improve it. Re-write what you said. Re-write what you thought. Re-write what you did.

5

Watch the re-written scene on the screen of your mind. Play out the new, improved episode in living Technicolor. Did your new version reflect the attitude of *To Lead Is To Serve?* If not, re-write it again.

9

Have Fun Everyday

∞

CHAPTER NINE

The joyous mood
is infectious
and brings success.
Intimidation may achieve
something momentarily,
but not for all time.
On the other hand,
when hearts are
won by friendliness
they will take on all
hardships willingly,
even death itself,
so great is the power
of joy over people.

I Ching

The ninth step is to have fun everyday.

The more seriously we take our work, the more important it is to be able to be light-hearted about it. If the *I Ching* is correct in saying that people will take on all hardships through joy, then the harder our work is, the more we need to lighten up. When others feel their work is hard, as the leader, we can serve them by sharing our own light-heartedness.

Conductor Zuben Mehta led the New York Philharmonic Orchestra through many challenges. He performed great music, serious music. Still, he remained light-hearted.

One day, comedian Danny Kaye asked the maestro if he could conduct the great orchestra. To the surprise of many, Mehta agreed. It was planned as a fund-raising event. Danny Kaye led the elated musicians through Beethoven, John Phillip Souza, and then performed a safety razor commercial! The familiar tune of the advertising jingle startled and delighted the listeners. Laughing and clapping, the enraptured audience granted them a standing ovation. Fundraiser Paula Root says the event grossed $335,000 for the Philharmonic and broadened the base of the orchestra's supporters.

Triumph with Humor

Humor is a great ally. It can prevent a brilliant leader from becoming arrogant with pride.

Arrogance drives volunteers away. Humor brings people together.

It is said that if we can look at a difficult person or at someone who really bothers us and laugh at ourselves and our attitude, we can touch the divine. If we cannot laugh, then we are stuck in our ego and pride. If we take ourselves too seriously, chances are that we have a huge ego, which will shatter sooner or later. In the meantime, it gets in the way of everything we want to do.

One year the partners in a large accounting firm invited the entire office to a luncheon. For entertainment, the senior partners dressed up and put on a fashion show. This was an outright reversal in what was expected from them and people still laugh when they recall the incident.

All things come to a person
who is modest and kind
in a high position.

Chinese Proverb

People give their support to leaders who are modest and kind, but enjoy bringing down those leaders who walk around with their noses up in the air. Isn't it true? It is the nature of the world. Nature wears down the mountains and fills in the valleys.

How to Climb the Ladder
of Success

When we remain humble on the ladder to success, we can climb as high as we want to go. As long as we can laugh at ourselves, we can continue to grow. When we start taking ourselves too seriously, we get into trouble.

A dynamic, young businesswoman was highly successful as a volunteer organizer in the Southwest. Soon leaders in her community began to talk about a future for her in politics. Newspaper articles were written about her. Then came the fall. Why? A friend said, "She started to believe her own P.R. She became impossible to work with and her future in politics was over before it ever got started."

The *I Ching* says, "If a leader allows himself to be dazzled by fame, he will soon be criticized. If, on the contrary, he remains modest despite his merit, he makes himself beloved and wins the support necessary for carrying his work through to the end."

If you want to find out about someone, give him a little power. Both his negative and positive qualities will be revealed. Power can lead us into arrogance. Therefore, as our power increases so must our accountability, responsibility, and light-heartedness. When we are in a leadership role, the spotlight is on us. That spotlight brings both our good deeds and our bad deeds into view. Whatever we do is illuminated; everyone watches. If we are full of pride and ambition, we become brittle and easily break. If we become arrogant, we bring about our own downfall.

On the other hand, if we approach our work with joy, we can do our best and stop worrying about the outcome. One way to let go of extreme ambition, pride, and desire is to pay attention when you notice those qualities in others. Ask yourself, "Do I do that?"

Every time you catch yourself noticing or judging someone else's ambition, pride and desire, point your finger in your own direction. Check yourself first. Then, if you are staring at your own reflection, ask yourself how you can act the opposite. This actually becomes an interesting and eventually enjoyable exercise as you begin to see people, who may have been difficult, warming up to you and your ideas. It also releases a lot of energy that can be used to have fun.

Let us go singing as far as we go;
the road will be less tedious.

Virgil

Laugh and Erase Your Stress

Laughter is the best medicine for letting go of stress. When we laugh, the whole body relaxes and we feel better physically and emotionally. Anxiety is released and the "big fun" replaces the "big problem."

I have a friend who is a professional musician. She says that when she was a child living in West Virginia she used to sing for hours in the garage, playing her guitar and pretending to entertain audiences. It was a lot of fun. After she became an entertainer by profession, all the joy went out of it. She began to take herself very seriously, causing extreme stress. She became heavy with ambition, pride, and desire. She was so focused on fame that she no longer enjoyed her work. After she realized this and let go of it, she once again enjoyed doing what she loves. She began to have fun again.

Have fun every day. Nothing attracts like a joyous heart. It is said, "Everybody loves a lover." People want to participate when we love what we are doing. They want to help. They respond from far, far away. On the other hand, if we are focused on how hard a project is, how much work there is, and how few people there are to do it, does anyone show up? Never! They run the opposite way.

I used to notice this on days when I felt lonely and tried to call a friend. Invariably, nobody was home. Yet, on days when I was full of enthusiasm and energy, my phone rang all day long with invitations. This proves to me that the energy we put out is what comes back to us.

We can serve our organization by putting out joyous energy. This is especially true when we have made a mistake. When we can admit our mistakes and be light-hearted about them, we grow. We are free to move on. Otherwise, we get stuck defending our position because the ego will do anything to justify itself.

You may ask, "What if the situation is not funny? What if it is intense?"

Have you ever noticed how the funniest movies are based on absolutely dreadful situations?

Sister Act, a film starring Whoopi Goldberg, is about a nightclub singer who unwillingly winds up in a convent. Taken seriously, it would be a miserable situation both for the singer and for the nuns. Can you imagine how the Mother Superior would cope with it? However, as a comedy, it is just this intensity and friction that make the movie so much fun.

To serve volunteers, let us see the comic side of intense situations and laugh. After all, what do we have to lose? Dreadful moments are so much fun to laugh about later. When we stop fighting the events in our lives, we get more than we had planned for. When we let our ideas about solutions go, we begin to grow. When we laugh at ourselves, we taste life, leadership, and that great force called "life's flow." Go with the flow. Laugh with the lot. When we stop fighting our situation, we have a lot more fun.

The funniest moments are often ordinary events. We do not have to tell jokes to be funny. We can simply notice the way things are. In *Crazy English*, author Richard Lederer does this with the English language in an exceptionally amusing way. He probes, "How can a slim chance and a fat chance be the same, while a wise man and a wise guy are opposites? How can the weather be hot as hell one day and cold as hell the next? You have to marvel at the unique lunacy of a language in which your house can burn up as it burns down, in which you fill in a form by filling it out and in which your alarm clock goes off by going on."

Lederer points out how delightfully funny things are.

We can, too.

GEMS to
REMEMBER

1

The joyous mood is infectious
and brings success.
The New York Philharmonic Orchestra.

2

Humor can prevent a leader
from becoming arrogant.
The accounting firm's fashion show.

3

People support a leader who
is modest and kind.
Mountains are worn down.

4

Laughter removes stress.
The musician from West Virginia.

5

If we allow ourselves to be dazzled by fame,
we will soon be criticized.

The woman who believed her own P.R.

6

If you want to find out about people, give
them a little power.

Do I do that?

7

Find humor in dreadful moments.

Whoopi Goldberg.

EXERCISE
for SUCCESS

1
Have fun today.

2
Do it again tomorrow.

10

Be Creative

℘

CHAPTER TEN

Good taste is

the enemy

of creativity.

Pablo Picasso

§

The tenth step is to be creative.

Creative ideas attract creative people. Creative organizations attract creative volunteers. Creativity can solve almost any dilemma. The challenge is to be open to it.

One definition for the word "create" is "to invest with a new form." No matter how great the Carousel Ball was last year and the year before, has it become merely another Carousel Ball? Does the project need to take on a new form? Creating new vehicles for volunteers will keep them inspired.

Are you looking for ways to increase the commitment of your volunteers?

Use your creativity.

As a staff member at the Hawaii State Judiciary, Earl Yonehara was searching for a way to inspire volunteers in the judicial system to commit to longer periods of service. He came up with the idea of offering each volunteer a judicial appointment. He had official appointment forms drawn up on old parchment paper and created a special ceremony that honors the commitment and generosity of the volunteers.

First, the volunteers attend a training program and then they attend a swearing-in ceremony with the Chief Justice of the State Supreme Court. They take an oath in which they solemnly swear to faithfully discharge their duties as citizen volunteers.

After that, they receive judicial appointments for a certain number of months or one year.

Earl's program has succeeded beyond his expectations. He notes that involving a top adminis-trator (in this case the Chief Justice) sends a message to the paid staff that the volunteers are important. Also, the definite time commitment makes it easier for the staff to invest time in training volunteers.

Pied pipers march outside the box. Look for creative ways to accomplish your goals and to include volunteers in the creative process. This keeps them interested and helps the organization to remain dynamic.

How To Be Creative

Once, I had a job in which I had to come up with a new idea every day. At first I thought, "This is impossible. How can I come up with something new every day?" I worried about it a lot. Then, one day it dawned on me that God comes up with a new day every day. Every sunrise is unique. Every moment is unlike the last. Every human face is different. If we are created in God's image, then we must have some of that creative ability, too.

After that insight, I changed. I did not magically come up with a new idea every day, but I no longer thought it was impossible. I knew it was possible.

According to a theory of aesthetics from Kashmir, creativity is born out of stillness. Kashmir lies in the foothills of the Himalayas, a snow covered mountain region rich in stillness. The theory is based on the oneness of all things and it holds that the initial creative impulse is a flash of awareness. In time, this awareness takes form. When it comes to a painter, it is envisioned as a painting; a sculptor sees a statue; an economist a new theory; an organizer a new format, and so on. The theory says that each creation is born complete and in time manifests as a tangible reality.

Artists know this. Michelangelo expressed his experience of this when he explained that as he looked at a piece of marble he saw the form already finished within it. His work was simply to chip away the outer casing. Artist Dan Warner says that he sometimes just sits and looks at a blank canvas for hours before he feels like painting. Other times, he pushes himself to begin. He works and works until something starts to unfold.

He says, "Then, magic arises and I'm in a different state. I am still and active at the same time. I'm painting automatically, and it's so easy. But up to that point, it is difficult.

"The magic doesn't happen with every painting, but when it does, I'm really pleased with the result.

I don't know what makes it happen. It is hard to say. A really nice feeling arises and I feel still."

To begin creating: first know that it is possible. Then be still. Then get started.

The artist must create a spark
before he can make a fire.

Auguste Rodin

Ria Keltz-Remenar, an artist who is also a realtor told me, "I learned from real estate that when nothing is happening, just do something. It doesn't really matter what it is, as long as I do something. Any action will cause a reaction. I applied this to my art and it gets me going every time."

Another artist who designs window displays at a department store says that when she first got her job, every time she changed a mannequin the dress would sell out of stock. Then she would have to change the display again. She got tired of changing the display so she started using dresses that she thought wouldn't sell. No luck! Eventually she realized that it had nothing to do with the dress. What mattered was taking action.

She says it is the same with her art. If she just does something (even clean the brushes) the energy begins to flow. Taking action is like breathing life into the project and letting something else take over.

"If you have a blank canvas, you have to put something on it," says Dan Warner. "Once you put something on it, then you have broken the spell. You have made the commitment. It's not just the commitment, though, it's the first action. Taking that first step is what does it."

There is a theory of aesthetics which defines a complete aesthetic experience as one that includes nine "rasas." In a loose sense, it could be called the nine flavors. These are: odious, terrible, erotic, heroic, comic, pathetic, furious, marvelous, and serene. According to this theory, art has to have all of these woven together to create a complete aesthetic experience.

Creativity is Versatility

So, how does all of this apply to being in charge of volunteers? It suggests a form of leadership. Do not get stuck in one style. Do not get stuck in terrible when you could easily be serene or comic when you should be forceful.

Use your creativity to find the right placement for even the most difficult person. In the hands of a great master, everything is of value. An artist has a lot of colors on the palette and an organization has a lot of different kinds of people. Like a good artist, the creative volunteer leader makes the best use of each one.

Be creative in the projects that you plan. Make some small and others enormous, some simple and some strenuous.

When making up a team to work together, the event will be more interesting if there are different flavors of people. Think of it as cooking. You would never plan a menu of all potatoes. Do not plan a committee of potatoes, either.

A master chef will balance a meal to include the five tastes: sweet, sour, salty, bitter and pungent. When we look at a project in this way, we see the value of having different kinds of people in the group. We may not like someone who is sour, but that person might be exactly what is required to balance the committee.

Setbacks Create Solutions

Successful creativity includes being creative with the resources that we have. Aren't the best cooks the ones who can go into the kitchen and whip up something with whatever is available?

You say you are not that kind of cook? You might not think that you are creative, but you do have setbacks, don't you?

The greatest creativity is often inspired by misfortune. Hemingway wrote about his anguish. Bill Cosby creates comedy out of adversity. Many of the most creative ideas on earth have come from calamity. Every great product is created in answer to a need and many, many noteworthy volunteer projects were born out of suffering.

Use setbacks to become creative. This is what management books refer to as being "proactive." Looking for solutions to your setbacks can lead to surprising successes.

The significant problems we have
cannot be solved with
the same level of thinking
with which we created them.

Albert Einstein

Dr. Sharon Miyashiro was organizing a women's rally for a senatorial candidate but interest was low. A few days before the event, it seemed like the rally would be a big dud. Then a florist friend called and said that someone had cancelled an order for 2,500 roses. Could Sharon think of any use for them?

She spent a few quiet moments thinking about how to use the roses. Her best memory was receiving one, which gave her an idea. She had to act quickly so she called on people who had helped her before. She telephoned six volunteers and sincerely said, "I need your help."

Sharon says, "They responded because it was a good cause and also because people want to be asked." The six were able to swiftly mobilize 30 volunteers. They came together to de-thorn each rose. They printed small tags announcing the women's rally and attached one to each rose with a yellow ribbon. At lunchtime, they went downtown and stood on the five busiest street corners passing out the roses.

Everyone wanted one. Secretaries were leaning out of office windows calling, "Save one for me!" A TV crew videotaped the rush for the roses. A newspaper printed a photo. The event went from a non-event to a grand success and many at the rally said they came because of the roses.

Sharon said that the 30 volunteers came right back asking, "What's next?"

She said, "Letting volunteers get a taste of success at an easy task is a terrific formula for involving them again in the future."

Man's mind stretched
to a new idea
never goes back to its original dimensions.

Oliver Wendell Holmes

Realtor Barbara Dew has been a volunteer for many organizations. She told me that a severe drop in membership was the catalyst for creative change in the Girl Scouts of America organization. The leadership asked experts at the Harvard School of Business for advice. They queried, "If we were a company losing clients, what would you recommend that we do?"

The Girl Scouts received some interesting counsel: even if you are a volunteer organization, you must run it like a business. Divide the leadership into two offices. One executive takes care of the nuts and bolts of managing and one is a public relations person for the organization. This executive should spend a lot of time at social events representing the Girl Scouts.

They were told to broaden their base and keep up with the times so as not to lose steam. As a result, the Girl Scouts began sponsoring "Space Camps" and programs that were entirely modern. At the same time, they devised a strategy to use nostalgia in their promotions. At large events they would ask, "If there is anyone here who was ever a Girl Scout, please stand up." Many women would stand and, of course, remember with fondness their Scouting days. This rekindled their enthusiasm for the Girl Scouts.

In this case, the drop in membership created a wonderful opportunity for regeneration. The organization used its problem to launch dynamic new programs.

You, too, can ask the experts for solutions. Also, you can take a good look at your organization. What does it have a lot of and what is it missing? Then use your creativity to use what you have to create what you need.

The Pennfield School in Wisconsin serves children with disabilities. They were having a capital fund drive and wanted to recruit celebrity help to raise money. An advertising agency suggested that they recruit some politicians.

At that time, the State of Wisconsin had eight living ex-governors. All eight were recruited and the school held a luncheon which included a tour of the school accompanied by the governors. The volunteers created a video showing the governors watching the children succeed in accomplishing small, difficult tasks. When the video was shown at the luncheon, there were few dry eyes in the crowd. One governor said, "I want to thank the women's movement for making it OK to cry at lunch today."

Enough money was raised to build a new wing onto the school. They named it "The Governor's Wing." Creatively, the fundraisers used what they had to create what was needed. Wisconsin had a lot of living ex-governors. The school needed money to expand. It was a perfect fit. As this illustrates, creativity can solve almost any dilemma as long as you are open to it.

For advice on fundraising, visit my website www.JoyofLeadership.com

GEMS to REMEMBER

1

Creative ideas attract creative people.
Volunteers being sworn in by the Chief Justice.

2

To get started with creativity,
just get started.
Artist cleaning her brushes.

3

Combine different flavors of people.
The committee of potatoes.

4

Creativity is often inspired by misfortune.
The rush for the roses.

5
Use a drop in membership as the catalyst for creative change.
Girl Scouts' Space Camps.

6
Create what you need from what you have.
The Wisconsin ex-governors.

EXERCISE
for SUCCESS

1
List the five things your organization
has a lot of.

2
List five things your organization
would like more of.

3
Ask people to find solutions to
#2 in list #1. For example:
Low interest in the rally and a lot of roses.
Few new Girl Scouts and many
former members.
The need for a celebrity sponsor and
having eight ex-governors.
Approach it like a game. Let children,
who are great at it, help.

11

Teams That Work

℘

CHAPTER ELEVEN

Power consists in
your capacity
to link your will
with the purpose
of others.

Woodrow Wilson

℘

The eleventh step is to create teams that work.

A dynamic team is like a beautiful bracelet. No matter how exquisite the jewels may be, they become a bracelet only when each gem is securely linked. As the leader of the team, our job is to be sure that all the links are secure. A pile of loose, individual gems is worth far less than a finely crafted piece of jewelry. In the same way, a lot of individual players are worth far less to your organization than a well-organized team.

Individual Work Is Weak – Team Work Is Strong

Look for ways to make the volunteers feel connected. When teamwork is strong, good ideas will bubble up to the surface. The leader's challenge is to link the individuals into a powerful team. The stronger the link, the more the group will be able to accomplish.

An Air Force officer told me how he begins building strong teams from the first day of orientation. On a blackboard he draws a diagram of all the jobs on the base. Every position is marked with an x. Then he points out where each person fits in.

"See that X there?" he says. "That is you, and your X is just as big as the commander's X. If you don't do your job, the commander can't do his."

The officer says that many of the new recruits do not consider their jobs to be important. They believe that the most important job in the Air Force is that of pilot. To these recruits the officer says, "Every job is essential. Your job makes it possible for others to do what they have to do. For instance, if you're in Finance, a pilot can't fly without you. You make sure his family gets a monthly check. When you do your job, it eases his mind. If he's worried, how will he concentrate on flying?"

The only thing that will redeem mankind is cooperation.

Bertrand Russell

You will dramatically improve your own experience of volunteer leadership when you start putting together strong teams. You'll accomplish more in less time, ease the burden of your responsibility and start having more fun.

A sensational example of this was illustrated by Sue King, a social worker who volunteered to organize the refreshments for her meditation organization. Eight events per month meant six people were needed to provide refreshments for each program. As chairperson, Sue needed to recruit 48 people every month to donate something good to eat.

The previous chairperson had become overwhelmed trying to recruit that many volunteers. As her overwhelm grew, fewer and fewer people volunteered to help. The refreshments were a disaster. Eventually she gave up recruiting and tried to bake most of the goodies herself. This was a huge task, so she quickly burned out and resigned.

When Sue accepted the position, within two weeks she had 48 volunteers contributing. This is how she did it: She broke it down into little steps. She made eight lists, one for each program. At the top of every list she wrote "Team Captain." Then she wrote numbers 1-6.

Team Captain: _____

1._____

2._____

3._____

4._____

5._____

6._____

Instead of recruiting all 48 people herself, she recruited eight team captains who were willing to be in charge once a month. They each recruited six people who would donate one refreshment a month. When the first woman was in charge, she and a couple of other people were begrudgingly doing everything. Under this plan, more than 48 people were happily participating.

One of the secrets of Sue's success was that, unknowingly, she applied the principle of *To Lead Is To Serve*. Sue continually served the team captains. If a captain could not find six people, she helped recruit them. Since she was not baking everything herself, she had time to talk with people at the programs and ask if they would like to participate. She constantly made the team captains feel supported.

Little By Little By Little

Another secret of Sue King's success was dividing the work into small increments. The first woman was trying to recruit 48 people. Sue was only looking for eight.

In the Bible, Nehemiah rebuilt the wall of Jerusalem in the same way. The wall around the city was its major protection. Today, a wall is not a primary defense system, but in Nehemiah's day, a wall was central to the city's safety. Rebuilding it was such a huge task that most people thought it couldn't be done. However, Nehemiah saw it another way. He divided the task into little sections, asking each person to be responsible for a small portion. The Bible describes in detail how each group rebuilt its own little part of the wall. In this way, the mission was accomplished quickly.

While reading about Nehemiah rebuilding the wall, I could envision each group doing its part with great enthusiasm. It reminded me of volunteer projects. They are always most successful when a lot of people do a little, as opposed to one or two people doing everything.

> *The journey of 1,000 miles*
> *begins with a single step.*
>
> Lao Tsu

The next time you face a project that seems big and overwhelming, approach it in this way: little by little by little. Divide the work into small steps. Any large project will be a great deal easier when it is divided into small endeavors.

Communicating Means Winning

"Communicating means winning" was the finding of an 18-month study by Dr. Jim Loehr of *Tennis Magazine*. Dr. Loehr says, "Talk is an extremely valuable way to improve your team's winning percentage."

In his research of amateur, college, and professional tennis doubles teams, Dr. Loehr studied the amount of communication between partners. The results were astonishing. At the pro level, partners talked between 83 percent of the points. The best college teams came together between 69 percent of the points.

But the amateur teams? They only talked between 17 percent of the points. In fact, amateurs communicated more to the opponents than with their partners.

The study reveals that the more professional a team is, the more it communicates. Dr. Loehr says, "Simply put, if you want to win, talk. It's especially important during the bad times. Great teams face adversity together, not individually."

Two tennis teams at Punahou School in Honolulu illustrate the value of good communication between teammates. There was a gold team and a blue team. The gold team was made up of the superstar tennis players. They were students who had taken lessons all their lives. They had the latest equipment and great outfits. Individually each member had beautiful strokes.

The blue team was made up of the students who enjoyed the game but who saw it as more of a pastime. They were enthusiastic about tennis, but they hadn't devoted a lot of energy to it. They neither had the skills nor the elaborate equipment of the gold team.

As the semester progressed, the blue team members always stayed to cheer on their teammates. Even though they were losing their matches, they would bring snacks and water and stay to encourage their teammates until the very last point was played. On the other hand, the gold team members would leave as soon as their individual matches were over.

In the middle of the semester something shifted and in the end, the blue team beat the gold team. Even though as individuals the blues were not the top players, their cohesiveness and teamwork made it possible for them to take the trophy.

Champion's Plan

Another strategy that supports strong teamwork is having a plan for adversity. Once we're far behind in the game, it's too late to call time-out and agree on how to handle it. But we can plan ahead. Dr. Loehr recommends five questions to ask your tennis partner before an adverse situation arises. We used the same five questions with workers in a volunteer agency that was undergoing a personnel turnover. The workers learned a lot about each other and grew stronger as a team through doing the exercise.

These are the five questions:

1. How can I help when you're nervous?
2. How should I react after you've made a dumb mistake?
3. How should I respond when you lose your temper?
4. How can I help when you're playing terribly (doing a bad job)?
5. How can I help when you're getting down on yourself?

Each person wrote their own answers. Then they reported aloud to the whole group. On Question #5, one woman said that when she got down on herself she wanted the others to tell her to throw that attitude out the window and move on. Within one hour, in another discussion, this woman did get down on herself by referring to her work as "pathetic." Two people in the group remembered her wish and said laughingly, "Throw it out the window and move on!" She hesitated for an instant, then joined in the laughter and moved on.

A note about this exercise: It brings out everyone's goodness. It makes the participants want to support each other. It also reveals that when we are not doing our best, we want other people's understanding instead of their criticism. Not one person said that they would be helped by the others telling them what they had done wrong.

Transform Your Team

Where there is friction, there is weakness. A bracelet will break if there is friction between two links. This is also true on a team. Find the weak links in your organization and strengthen them, or the work will suffer. Assist the parts to cooperate for the benefit of the whole. When people are having difficulties getting along with one another, sometimes all it takes is for them to sit down and talk. When they resolve their differences through communication, the friction often transforms into tremendous creative energy.

Teams that work are like beautiful bracelets. As a volunteer leader, keep in mind that each person is a jewel. Take care of everyone like a precious gem and you will develop a strong and solid team.

GEMS to
REMEMBER

1
Individual work is weak. Teamwork is strong.
Loose gems vs. a bracelet.

2
Every job is essential. Each job makes it possible for others to do what they have to do.
The Air Force captain.

3
Break it down into small steps.
Sue King and the refreshments;
Nehemiah and the wall.

4
Communicating means winning.
Tennis doubles partners.

5

Teamwork wins.

The blue team and the gold team.

6

Strong teams plan for adversity.

How can I help?

7

Where there is friction between people,
the work becomes weak.

A great team is like a beautiful bracelet.

EXERCISE
for SUCCESS

1

Write down a sizeable task that you face.

2

Name three to eight people who could be
team captains for this task.

3

What will each team captain be
expected to do?

4

How many people would each captain
need to recruit?

5

What would each person be expected to do?
E.g., bake a refreshment once a month.

6

Sit down with your team and go through
the five questions, *How Can I Help?*
If the team is large, divide into smaller
groups of people who work
closely together.

12

Letting Go

℘

CHAPTER TWELVE

To attain knowledge,
add things
every day.
To attain wisdom,
remove things
every day.

Lao Tsu

℘

The twelvth step is to let go.

Sometimes the best way we can serve volunteers is to let them go.

I used to have a volunteer assistant whom I relied on tremendously. She was dependable, organized, and loyal. However, she was not blossoming in her position. She was qualified to handle more responsibility but, because I felt so dependent on the support that she gave me, I wasn't thinking of her growth. I was not serving her. More than once my supervisor hinted that she should move on, but I couldn't let her go. I depended on her too much. Finally, my supervisor offered her a better position.

When she left the office, another volunteer replaced her. This man was also dependable and organized. In addition, he was tremendously creative. With his help our work flourished and the department grew. So did the woman who had left. She went on to a position in which she was able to shine.

The lesson for me was, and I offer it to you: When it is time to let go, it is time to let go.

Let Whoever Comes Come, and Whoever Goes Go

It is said that if something truly belongs to you it cannot be lost, even if you throw it away. So don't hold on to people too tightly and do not worry.

Welcome people and let them know that they are appreciated. Listen to them and offer challenging, creative volunteer projects. If after a period of time they do not thrive then let them go. When an orchid is in its proper soil, it will bloom. If the soil isn't right, no matter how much attention the orchid receives, it will not flourish.

Holding onto a volunteer is like holding onto sand. If you squeeze it tightly you may be surprised to see that only half the grains remain in your hand. The rest flow out between your fingers. But if you gently cradle the sand in your open hand, every grain will stay.

In the same way, when you hold on to people too tightly, you will lose them.

Have you ever squeezed volunteers? Or do you cradle them loosely? Clinging to volunteers too tightly will scare them away.

How to Let a Volunteer Go

What happens when volunteers don't want to leave but we want to let them go?

Approach the situation with the attitude of service to the organization and to the volunteer. If someone is having difficulty in a position and it is obvious that it's time for her to move on, you are actually doing her a favor to address the situation.

Mary Jane Anaya of the Kauai Non-Profit Resource Center says that she has had success in following the advice of the *One Minute Manager*. When she knows that she needs to let someone go, she begins by asking, "Do you feel that you are doing the very best that you can in this position?"

"No one ever answers yes," she says. "They know that they are not doing well, even if at first they don't feel safe in admitting it."

Then Mary Jane asks, "What do you think we ought to do about it?"

She says, "They fire themselves. Usually they say, 'I shouldn't be in this position. I don't like this kind of work. I thought I would, but I don't.'"

She advises that when an employee or a volunteer departs, "Do not talk stink behind anyone's back. It always gets back to them. Let them leave with decorum and self-esteem. Then they have something good to say about your organization. Call them in privately. Appreciate them. Thank them. Protect their dignity as much as you can."

Imozelle McVeigh is a Director of Volunteer Services at a large hospital near San Diego, California. She oversees 800 adult and 320 youth volunteers. Imozelle has learned that when you have to fire a volunteer, it is best to put it in writing. "I had a volunteer I needed to replace as an area chairperson," she recalls. "I did it verbally at first and he just didn't get it. I thought I was clear, but he didn't understand and complained to my boss.

"My boss called me and insisted, 'I've got Carl in my office complaining about you. Take care of him, but you have to let him go.'

"So I wrote a letter to Carl," Imozelle says. "I outlined exactly what had happened: 'I asked you to write a job description. You didn't. I asked you to call a meeting of the group. You didn't. I asked you to come to the hospital in the proper dress. You wore a plaid shirt. Our policy is a white shirt.' I spelled out all the reasons I had to replace him as the chairperson."

"A week later, I ran into him and he said, 'I owe you an apology.'

"I said, 'No, I owe you an apology because I wasn't clear the first time.' Almost in unison, we both said, 'It's all forgotten.'"

The man resigned as chairperson and understood why he was asked to step down. No one had ever told him what was expected of him, nor pointed out that he wasn't achieving it. He continued to volunteer and has flourished. In fact, he and Imozelle have become good friends and he often brings her pictures of his grandchildren. Imozelle points out that she learned a valuable lesson in this experience: always let a volunteer know what is expected of him.

She recommends that when you have to let volunteers go, put it in writing in the form of a letter. They can read it alone, in their own time, when they are calm and can reflect on why they are being fired.

> *Take hold lightly;*
> *let go lightly.*

Spanish Proverb

Another time Imozelle had to let a volunteer go for violating a hospital rule. The hospital has a policy against selling things on the hospital grounds and the volunteer was making little booties and selling them to the visitors in the lobby. The first two times it happened, Imozelle gave the volunteer verbal warnings, saying, "Please don't."

The third time, she handed her a letter: "I have told you and you continue to do this. You can no longer volunteer in the lobby."

Imozelle says, "You have to do this for the good of your volunteer program. If other volunteers see someone breaking rules and getting away with it, what does that say to them? What credibility do you have?"

How to Let Go of Long-Term Volunteers

To let new volunteers go is relatively easy. Call them in and point out, "You may not be cut out for this." As Mary Jane said above, they often fire themselves when given a chance to talk about it.

It is more difficult to let someone go who has been volunteering for years and years. She may have been a wonderful volunteer in the past but, for whatever reason, she isn't doing the job well anymore. This is a tough challenge. Again, call her in privately. Protect her dignity as much as you can. As nicely as possible, spell out the requirements of the position that she is not fulfilling.

Of course, you don't say, "You just can't volunteer here anymore." Instead say, "I have seen that you are forgetting appointments. I have seen that you are not answering the phones properly anymore." Give specific examples that she will recognize. With some volunteers, you have to keep repeating your observations over and over.

If she says, "Nope! I'm doing just fine," don't argue. Simply say what you have observed.

With a troublemaker or a volunteer who is argumentative, use the same procedure. Say, "This is what I have heard. So and so has reported that you are being difficult." You have to spell it out very clearly that this behavior is not acceptable.

It is good to give warnings. The first time say, "Please don't do that again." If the volunteer continues the behavior after one or two more warnings, you have to treat it like a firing situation. Just like working with employees, go through the steps before you actually fire the person. Emphatically state, "This is not acceptable behavior." Six months later, if the inappropriate behavior has not changed, you have to let him go.

Another possible solution is to move the volunteer into a different position. Say, "We are going to re-structure and need you to do a different job."

One Director of Volunteers overheard a volunteer in the main lobby of a hospital say, "I would never come to this hospital."

The director said to the volunteer, "I can't have you working in the main lobby." She was moved to the outpatient department where she worked with patients instead of visitors.

The director says, "She is wonderful there. They love her in that department where she makes up beds for the patients. They don't care that she is a little bit outspoken. The staff is nurturing and she likes that. They celebrate her birthday and tell her, "Mary, we are so glad you came today."

This volunteer was hurt that she couldn't work in the lobby, but it worked out well in the end.

Sometimes it's only a matter of finding the right niche for people who are difficult.

Some leaders find that they are more comfortable when letting a volunteer go if they take someone else along. A second party can offer a different perspective and lend support. This is especially important if the person who is being let go tends to be angry or violent. No matter how experienced we are, it can be difficult to give out bad news.

On the other hand, it could be intimidating and heavy-handed for two people to confront a volunteer with disappointing news. This has to be done very gently, keeping in mind the goal of serving the organization and the volunteer.

How to Thrive by Letting Go of Pride

If employees or volunteers are choosing to leave because they are upset with your organization, ask those who are leaving to tell you their reasons. When a plant begins dying, gardeners have to look at the fertilizer they are using, as well as the water, air, and soil. If several plants die, something is wrong. When several volunteers leave, something is definitely wrong. Stay open to hearing what they have to say.

I used to volunteer for a thriving organization. A new volunteer director came on board and soon afterwards many people stopped volunteering. Donations went down. The public stopped attending our events. The volunteer director pointed the finger of blame in many directions – not at herself. She refused to look at her own behavior. She actually refused to discuss the dwindling participation, which had dropped by sixty percent. She didn't ask why people were leaving because she couldn't face the fact that it had something to do with her. Her pride prevented her from growing as a leader.

Do not play ostrich. Ask for honest evaluations. Set aside self-importance and sincerely question, "What do we need to change?" Then make the changes and grow from what you receive. This will benefit the volunteers, the leaders, and the organization's mission.

When I speak of letting go, I also mean that we have to let go of bad habits that we have developed in dealing with volunteers. One common habit is manipulation by guilt – using guilt as a motivator. For example, when a supervisor with a limited volunteer force creates the impression that if the volunteers don't go the extra mile the project will fail. She implies that the volunteers just aren't committed enough or they need to put in more hours. This is manipulation by guilt.

Let it go. Guilt creates stagnation. A leader using guilt on volunteers is like a gardener pouring poison on the plants. Guilt kills energy and enthusiasm. It creates resentment, so never try to make anyone feel guilty. If volunteers are doing the work out of guilt, how effective can they be? A poisoned plant cannot bloom. On the other hand, when we let go of guilt, it leaves room for enthusiasm.

We can also let go of rigid procedures and complicated systems for advancement.Rather than insist that people stay in the same position endlessly, we can give them experience in different areas. Letting people move around within the organization will help you to keep good volunteers. Also, letting people who get along well with each other work together creates an atmosphere of trust and camaraderie which benefits everyone.

After Letting Go

After volunteers have been let go, forgive and forget. Gossip and office politics are the last things a volunteer organization needs. Clear the air and move on. As soon as you do, the organization will begin to feel healthy and functional again.

When I was holding onto my assistant, I was not only holding her back, I was also holding my organization back. When the time has come to let go, avoiding it stunts the growth of all concerned. Growth is natural. So is pruning. So is letting go.

GEMS *to* REMEMBER

໑

1

Serve volunteers by letting
them go and grow.
Shar's assistant.

2

Make sure volunteers know what is
expected of them.
Imozelle McVeigh's experience.

3

If people are not thriving, move them to a
different position.
An orchid in its proper soil blooms.

4

Put it in writing.
The chairperson at the hospital.

5
Ask those who are leaving to point out what your organization is doing wrong.
The sixty percent decline.

6
Let go of guilt.
*Pruning and growth are part
of the natural cycle.*

EXERCISE
for SUCCESS

1
Do I let people do what they do best?

2
Do I let volunteers know what is expected of them?

3
Do I make people feel guilty?

4
What will I do to change?

13

Reaching Our Goals

℘

CHAPTER THIRTEEN

The moment one
definitely commits oneself,
then Providence
moves too.

Goethe

℘

The final step is to reach our goals.

By now you may be saying, "I have tried all of these things. I believe in this. I am like the king in the Talmud. I meet people halfway, but it doesn't always work. Too many things get in the way."

My response is, "How do you think Thomas Edison felt?"

Thomas Edison made 10,000 attempts to invent the light bulb. Someone asked him, "How did it feel to fail 10,000 times?"

He replied, "I did not fail. I learned 10,000 ways that it would not work."

Edison refused to call his 10,000 attempts "failures." Rather, he saw them as 10,000 lessons learned. How many "lessons" will we learn?

There is a principle of social physics that goes like this: *The degree of success is proportional to the number of obstacles overcome.*

Gold becomes pure by being subjected to fire. A muscle gets strong from repeated resistance. In the same way, people and projects succeed after repeated trials and errors.

You Cannot Fail

Many years ago I was an entertainment reporter in Hollywood. The awards shows always gave recognition to the best new artist, best new group, etc. I would often interview the "Best New Star" only to find out that he or she had been in the business for 10 or 15 years! The "new success" came after years of what some would call failures but that we call lessons. The creative artists had learned another principle of social physics: *You cannot fail unless you quit.*

Why would we quit?

Fear. Fear stops us. Fear of what people think. Fear of whether or not we can accomplish our goal.

Will I succeed?

Will I look foolish?

Am I capable of doing this?

Have I taken on more than I can handle?

Is it worth it?

Fear causes paralysis. Look at what happens to our bodies when we become afraid. We stop breathing, our muscles tighten, our heartbeat quickens, we break out in a sweat.

Once, I was skiing in Sun Valley, Idaho and found myself in a class that was much more daring than I was ready for. Most of the time we were on steep slopes that scared me to death. However, we had a great instructor who told us something I will never forget. He said, "Keep your eyes on the distance. Look at the skyline and the beautiful mountains. Keep looking ahead. When you see yourself as part of the big picture, everything appears to be moving very slowly. On the other hand, if you look down at your feet, you appear to be moving so fast that you think you are out of control."

When you get scared, keep your eyes on the big picture.

Attract Support by Setting A Goal

When we set a goal, it draws support from others. The New York Philharmonic set a monetary goal for a three-day radiothon. For 72 hours they continually announced the goal over the radio. As it neared the end and the goal had not been reached, public support began to roll in. Even a cab driver called in with a pledge saying, "You've got to meet that goal or I'm gonna give you all my tips!"

Spectators love to cheer at the finish line. People's good wishes support an athlete and they help an organization. One reason people love to play games is that games have clearly defined goals and human beings enjoy reaching a target. When we set a clear goal, people are inspired to give their time, money, and good wishes to help us attain it. When we realize the goal, it makes people happy.

Setting a clear goal helps volunteers remain committed, especially if they work alone. Let them know 95 envelopes need to be addressed or that

25 members need to be contacted today. There is a certain type of volunteer who can't quit until the project is completed. A clearly defined, achievable goal will keep that person working until the very end.

By the way, the New York Philharmonic did meet that goal.

To Hit the Target, Constantly Keep the Goal In Sight

*If the trumpet does not
sound a clear call,
who will get ready for battle?*

Corinthians

In sports, more spectators attend games in which they can see a goal line, such as football, soccer, and horse racing. Fewer people go to watch long distance running. To accomplish anything, we must constantly keep the goal in sight. When we do, we're more likely to reach it. Goals also entice volunteers to help us.

As the leader, we can serve volunteers by helping them to keep the goal in sight at all times. Never let them forget why they are volunteering. Constantly cheer them on toward the goal line and gently correct them when they get off course, reminding them of the direction the team is taking.

Many things come up in every organization, including complicated relationships, pride, and power struggles. These are like the bumps and setbacks that football players experience on the field. But when the running back crosses the goal line with 80,000 people cheering, all those hard knocks become just a part of the game. The player usually cannot wait to get back out on the field.

It is the same with volunteers. We can help them endure the bumps and knocks of volunteering by making the goal line very clear and continually pointing them toward it.

To Boost Your Success, Write the Goal Down

A study was done of Harvard graduates. A decade after graduation, the alumni were asked about their accomplishments. The study found that those who had a goal in mind at graduation were three times more successful than those who had no goal. The ones who had set a goal and written it down had been *10 times* more successful.

In one of our *To Lead Is To Serve* seminars on "How to Attract Volunteers and Keep Them," we had just introduced this information about writing down your goal when a participant raised her hand

and asked if she could say something to the group. She was from a local chapter of the American Diabetes Association where we had given the workshop a year earlier. She shared that before her chapter began writing down its goals, the most money the organization had ever raised in one year was $70,000. After the workshop, the volunteers set a $100,000 goal, then posted it for all to see. They raised $121,000 – a 58% increase!

Putting a goal in writing makes it easier to focus on. Post the goal and keep it right in front of you at all times. If it is sitting on your desk staring you in the eye when the phone rings with an interesting diversion, looking at the goal will make it easier to say, "Not now." Looking at the written goal when you are planning the day or the week helps, too. What percentage of time are you investing in what you truly wish to achieve?

To Make it Easy, Make a Plan

Make a specific plan for reaching the goal. Your plan becomes your road map. By following your map, the chances of reaching your chosen destination are infinitely greater than if you travel with only a vague notion of where you are going. Even a crude map is better than none. Even a crude plan for reaching a goal will be more successful than no plan.

Don't forget: It is in giving that we receive. What amount of time and effort are you willing to give in exchange for achieving the goal? What quality of work will you do? This needs to be included in the plan.

About Obstacles

We must understand an important point about obstacles: They are there for a reason. Behind every obstruction is a great opening, a great opportunity. Obstacles are there to teach us something, to change our direction, to hold us back for awhile until the time is right. They are even there to protect us.

A successful developer was planning to build 125 condominiums on the Hawaiian island of Kauai. He had bought the property, hired a contractor, and was ready to go. However, he could not get a permit. For three years his permit application was denied even though the housing was needed. In fact, Kauai had a housing shortage. The condos were modestly priced. They were environmentally planned. Still, he could not get the permit.

Then a hurricane hit Kauai. Fifty per cent of the buildings on the island were damaged or destroyed. Since he had not gotten the permit, his had never been built. What he had thought was an obstacle had protected him.

In Nagasaki, Japan, there is a mountain lookout for tourists. From the lookout it is possible to see the entire section of the city that was destroyed by the atomic bomb. The guide explains that the only people who survived the attack were those who lived on the other side of the mountain. When I heard this, I could not help thinking that before the bomb some people must have seen the mountain as an obstacle to cross whenever they wanted to go into the city or to the shore. At the time of the bombing, however, the mountain obstacle saved their lives.

This is how obstacles can be. When a bone breaks, if it is properly set, it grows back stronger. It is possible that your obstacles are there to make you resilient. So when you find yourself face to face with a big obstruction, do not become discouraged. Later, you may change your point of view.

*As long as we stand
in our own way,
everything seems to be
in our way.*

Ralph Waldo Emerson

A Technique for Reaching Your Goals

A technique for reaching your goals is to follow the example of water. Water reaches its goal by flowing on.

What does water do when it comes upon a rock? It flows over or around it. When it comes to a precipice does it squeal, "On no! That's much too steep for me?" No. It goes right over the cliff. Does it hesitate even for a second? What happens when it comes to a hole? It fills the hole up and flows on.

On the other hand, what occurs when water does not move on? It gets stagnant, doesn't it? It is the same with us. If we let fear or indecision stop us, we stagnate, too.

The technique of flowing on like water works especially well when we are afraid to make a decision. How many times have we been afraid to act? How many times has fear left us frozen like a lizard? When we are afraid, the worst thing we can do is nothing.

No matter what the situation is, after it has been thoroughly thought out, it is essential to make a decision and to act. When we do not act, we get stuck. At these times, we can remember the example of water and flow on.

Look at any form of running water. Fix your gaze on a fountain. Sit at the seashore. Lie on a river bank. Walk in the rain. Learn to be like water, continuously flowing on.

Water dissolves things. Let it dissolve your obstacles. If you do not have a natural source of water nearby, then turn on a garden hose. Use a faucet. Get in the shower. Stare at running water and move on.

Staring at flowing water helps us bypass the old part of our thinking that is stuck. It helps us get in touch with the part of us that is free and liquid.

When Thomas Edison met with 10,000 obstacles in his quest to invent the light bulb, 10,000 times he moved on. In the same way, no matter how discouraged you may be, there is a place inside that has mobility. Behind every obstruction is a great opening, a great opportunity. Let running water lead you there.

Give generously.
Water gives without asking to be repaid.

Speak faithfully,
like the flow of water that always
goes toward the sea.

Govern gently.
Though water moves with gentleness,
it can overcome even the hardest obstacle.

Be adaptable.
Water can fit what is square or what is round.

Take action opportunely.
Water freezes in the winter and melts in the spring.

Ni, Hua Ching

The Book of Changes and the Unchanging Truth
College of Tao and Traditional Chinese Healing, Publisher

GEMS *to*
REMEMBER
$\wp$

1

The degree of success is proportional to the
number of obstacles overcome.
Thomas Edison.

2

You cannot fail unless you quit.
The "Best New Stars."

3

When you get scared, keep your eyes
on the big picture.
Skiing in Idaho.

4

Setting a clear goal draws the support
of others.
New York Philharmonic.

5
Write the goal down.
Harvard graduates.

6
Obstacles may be there for a reason.
Kauai housing shortage and Nagasaki.

7
Follow the example of water.
Water reaches its goal by flowing on.

EXERCISE
for SUCCESS

ℒ

1
Write your goal at the top of a blank
sheet of paper.

2
Make a list of reasons why achieving this
goal will benefit you and others. Make the
reasons convincing enough to convince
yourself. Remember: *To Lead Is To Serve.*
What will you give in return?

3
Draw three circles under the goal. In each
circle, write one obstacle that lies between
you and your goal.

4
Go to the ocean, a stream, a lake, a river,
a waterfall, any form of flowing water.
Mentally place your obstacles in the water.

5

Spend 10 minutes staring at water. Then use this memory in the future. Whenever you run up against an obstacle, ask yourself, "What would water do now?"

6

Post your personal goals in a place where you can see them every day. Post the goals of the organization in a place where everyone can see them.

7

A great river begins with a drop of water. Even the most enormous project begins with one small step. What step will you take today toward reaching your goal?

Index

Thank you for reading
To Lead Is To Serve.
Thank you for the service you
offer to the world.
It is said that when one person
turns toward love,
the whole earth rejoices.
Because of you,
life on our planet has changed
for the better.

Shar McBee

For advice on fundraising, visit my website www.JoyofLeadership.com

To Lead Is To Serve

ORDERING INFORMATION
℘

FREE weekly email leadership tip
Subscribe at:
www.toleadistoserve.com

To Lead Is To Serve
book discounts
10 or more books – 10% off
25 or more books – 25% off
100 + books – 42% off
Call 1.800.814.8827

To Lead Is To Serve
Audio Book
CD – $19.95

"Learn by Phone"
Courses
Why travel when you can learn in the comfort of your home or office? Our courses are taught over the telephone. Students call in from around the world for these interactive, inspiring sessions. Read about the courses and register at www.toleadistoserve.com

Become a Certified
To Lead Is To Serve
Seminar Leader
If you are an experienced volunteer leader, you may apply for our certification through the *To Lead Is To Serve* website.

Will Shar McBee be in your area?
Are you looking for a keynote speaker?
You can book Shar McBee for a speaking engagement or locate a Certified Seminar Leader.
www.toleadistoserve.com.

Prices do not include shipping. To place your orders and to register for courses online visit our website.

www.toleadistoserve.com